THE BASKETBALL CLINIC'S

TREASURY OF DRILLS

THE BASKETBALL CLINIC'S

TREASURY

OF DRILLS

Compiled by the Editors of

THE BASKETBALL CLINIC

Parker Publishing Company, Inc.
West Nyack, New York

©1977, *by*

PARKER PUBLISHING COMPANY

West Nyack, N.Y.

Library of Congress Cataloging in Publication Data
Main entry under title:

The Basketball clinic's treasury of drills.

   1. Basketball--Training. I. Basketball clinic.
II. Title: Treasury of drills.
GV885.35.B37   796.32'32   76-45413
ISBN 0-13-072264-2

Printed in the United States of America

Introduction

Here are some of the best basketball drills selected from over 650 articles that have appeared in our monthly publication, *The Basketball Clinic*.

Thirty-five of basketball's most successful high school and college coaches combine to demonstrate (with over 160 illustrations) their drill programs for perfecting individual and team skills.

You'll find drills for warm-ups and conditioning, tailor-made offensive and defensive drills, multiple-purpose drills to fit any style of play, and drills for pre-season and post-season training. Whether you're a first-year coach or an established veteran, this book is certain to become one of your most valuable tools in building a winning basketball program.

Board of Editors
THE BASKETBALL CLINIC

ALSO FROM THE EDITORS OF THE BASKETBALL
CLINIC:

A Coaching Treasury from the Basketball Clinic. Parker
Publishing Company, Inc., 1974.

CONTENTS

Introduction 5

PART I   OFFENSIVE DRILLS

1. **Fundamental Offensive Drills for Basketball Success**

   by Bob Basarich 15

2. **Drills to Perfect Shooting**

   by John J. Rodgers 23

3. **Shooting Drills: Theories And Practices**

   by Robert L. Metcalf 29

4. **Pressure Free-Throw Drills**

   by Gene Snell 37

5. **Drills for Teaching Rebounding**

   by Charles A. Field 43

6. **All-Purpose Dribbling Drill**

   by Chic Hess 51

7. Dribbling Drills With the "Dribble Aid"

by Virgil Sweet 57

8. A Dribbling and Ball-Handling Series

by Mike Tramuta 61

9. Ball-Handling Drills to Develop a Player's Full Potential

by Harley "Skeeter" Swift and Clay Estes 67

10. Ball-Handling Drills to Develop Quickness

by Hank Fengler 77

11. An All-Purpose Offensive Drill: The Falcon Frolic

by Joseph E. Flannery 85

12. An All-Purpose Drill for the Fast Break

by Phil Faulkner 93

PART II DEFENSIVE DRILLS

1. Drills to Develop Sound Defensive Fundamentals

by Raymond Zsolcsak 101

2. Basic Drills for Tough Defensive Play

by Ed Higginbotham 107

3. Defensive Drills to Perfect Fundamentals

by Billy Allgood 113

4. Drills to Teach Defense

by Bart Talamini 119

5. **Drills for Developing an Aggressive Defensive Attitude**

   by Jim Mogan **129**

6. **Drills to Master Defensive Game Situations**

   by Paul J. Frey **137**

7. **Drills for Improving Individual Defensive Skills**

   by Bill Leatherman **145**

8. **Teaching Defensive Know-How With Breakdown Drills**

   by Mike Schrecongost **151**

9. **Defensive Position: Ideas and Drills**

   by Johnny A. McCalpine **161**

10. **Defensive Drills for a Feeder System**

    by George Noch **167**

PART III   CONDITIONING DRILLS

1. **A Physical Development Program for Basketball Success**

   by Ray Landers **177**

2. **Basic Conditioning Drills**

   by H. W. Thistlewaite **191**

3. **Combining Conditioning and Skill Drills**

   by Bill Hill **197**

4. **Conditioning: Key to Modern Basketball**

   by Nick Creola **203**

5. **Drills to Condition the Individual**

   by Dave Hadaway .... .207

6. **Conditioning Drills for Fundamental Play**

   by Peter Mathiesen .... .215

7. **A Pre-Season Conditioning Circuit**

   by Donald M. Jackson .... .223

8. **Pre-Season Training Ideas for the Small School**

   by Anthony Zanin .... .227

9. **Pre-Season and Early-Season Basketball Preparation**

   by Lenny Fant .... .233

10. **An Off-Season Workout Program**

    by Bob Whitehead .... .239

11. **A Summer Training Program**

    by Oscar Catlin .... .243

12. **Basketball Drills: Conditioners for the Game**

    by Woody Williams .... .247

THE BASKETBALL CLINIC'S

TREASURY OF DRILLS

PART I

OFFENSIVE DRILLS

Bob Basarich

Head Basketball Coach
Central High School
Lockport, Illinois

FUNDAMENTAL OFFENSIVE DRILLS FOR BASKETBALL SUCCESS

Bob Basarich has been coaching high school basketball for a number of years. As head basketball coach at Central High School, he has compiled a most impressive three-year record of 77 wins against 9 losses (24-5; 28-2; 25-2).

Like most coaches, we have some favorite drills that do the job for us in our basketball program. They are fundamental drills but most important for continued success. They are as follows:

- Passing drill.
- Four-corner drill.
- Dribbling-chair drill.
- Combination drill.
- Fast-break reaction drill.

Note: The first four are not original with us, but we have changed them a bit from the usual. The fast-break reaction drill is our own as far as we know.

PASSING DRILL

It is set up as shown in Diagram 1. The passes are: (1) two-hand over the head; (2) two-hand chest pass; (3) two-hand bounce pass; (4) outlet baseball pass using hand to outside; (5) flip or drop pass; (6) one-hand bounce pass; (7) hook pass using hand to outside.

> Note: Man receiving pass 1 becomes outlet man. Man receiving pass 2 becomes rebounder. Players rotate from left to right—line A to B, B to C, C to A. After all players shoot right-handed, reverse drill and shoot left-handed.

FOUR-CORNER DRILL

It is set up as shown in Diagram 2: (1) Make sure lines are as even as possible; (2) player lines are in the four corners of half-court; (3) ball begins with A; (4) A passes to B using two-hand over the head pass; (5) after A passes to B he breaks around B, then to basket for eventual return pass and lay-up; (6) B passes to C using the two-hand chest pass; (7) C passes to D using two-hand bounce pass; (8) D feeds A for the layup using bounce pass or flip; (9) after B passes to C, B goes to free-throw line to wait pass from rebounder—D, person who feeds shooter, rebounds and passes to B at free-throw line—B then pivots and passes back out to A's line and drill begins for next group of four; (10) after performing drill, players rotate lines and do so by running around out-of-bounds lines—this allows the drill to run continuously with no delay.

> Special Points: (1) After every player has shot right-handed layup, ball starts with B and goes the other way (to A) and B shoots left-handed layup; the entire drill is reversed (Diagram 3); (2) rotation of lines is performed by going to line your first pass was thrown to; (3) "A" should time himself so that he receives pass for layup at full speed; (4) every player waits in corner until ball is ready to be thrown to him—then breaks out to receive pass; after receiving ball, player pivots

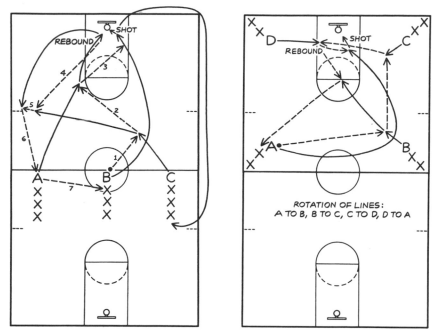

Diagram 1

Diagram 2

ROTATION OF LINES:
A TO B, B TO C, C TO D, D TO A

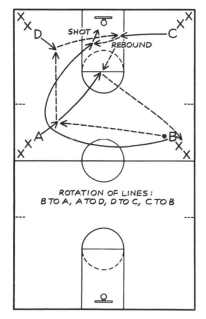

Diagram 3

ROTATION OF LINES:
B TO A, A TO D, D TO C, C TO B

and makes sharp pass to next player; (5) when players are good at running drill, use two balls—second ball does not start until first ball is being shot for layup.

DRIBBLING-CHAIR DRILL

Place chairs as shown in Diagram 4—about three feet off lane and circle. Start line in left corner of floor and all players have a ball if possible. Dribble to first chair, make full turn and drive around chairs, staying as close as possible. Second time through follow set-up shown in Diagram 5—weave through chairs switching hands. Third time through follow Diagram 6—circling each chair, using outside hand and pretending chair is an opponent. After squad has gone through from left corner, switch to right side of floor and run the three again.

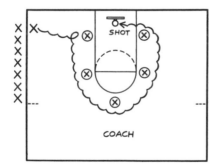

Diagram 4

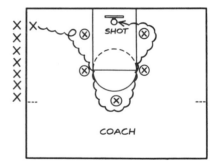

Diagram 5

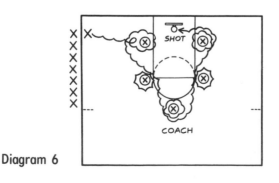

Diagram 6

Points of Importance: All dribbling must be done at a speed at which the player can control the ball. Chairs are considered as defensive players—therefore, the dribbler always protects the ball. A layup is attempted at the end of each circling of the chairs. Coach holds an arm straight out giving a numerical sign with one hand—as the player dribbles past or around the chair at the top of the circle, he yells out the number of fingers the coach held up. On last drill (Diagram 6), have second player wait until first player is at third chair before beginning—this is to avoid collisions.

COMBINATION DRILL

This drill is illustrated in Diagrams 7 and 8. First player in center line positions himself on dotted line—throws the ball against the board and rebounds. He then passes out to either line (Diagram 7). Player that receives pass from line 1 takes ball to the center lane by dribbling and continues dribbling until he gets to free-throw line or is picked up by the defense.

Player from line 1 fills in lane 2 or 3 depending on line he passed to. Players have now reached scoring area and have 3-on-2 situation. Player with ball is at free-throw line. Players in outside lanes stop below free-throw line at angle to basket. If they get the ball they are in position to use the board when shooting. The three offensive players continue to shoot until they score or the defense gets the ball.

Note: When defense gets the ball, they fast break back, bringing about a 2-on-1 situation. The man on defense is the first man in center line. Players rotate from left to right. Player who started in line 3 comes back and other two stay on defense (Diagram 8).

FIRST-BREAK REACTION DRILL

The drill is set up as shown in Diagram 9—3 lines are used, A, B and C—two balls are used and start in lines A and B or C and B. Players never dribble. Line B begins drill by

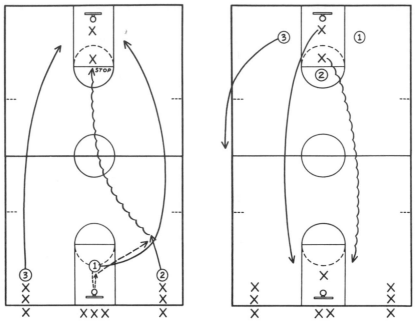

Diagram 7

Diagram 8

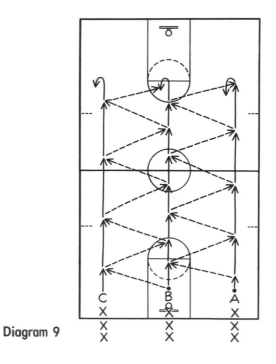

Diagram 9

passing to line C. As soon as B passes to C, line B turns head and looks for pass from A. As soon as B receives pass from A, B returns a pass to A—then turns head and is ready for pass from C.

Note: One ball must always be in center line at start of drill.

After reaching free-throw line at far end of floor, players turn and follow same pattern coming back. Players rotate lines from left to right.

Note: Reasons for the drill are: being able to pass on the run without dribbling; reaction to ball and looking for the lane that is open; weighted basketballs may be used, of course, and this would help build stronger wrists and arms.

2   John J. Rodgers

Head Basketball Coach
Harrison High School
Harrison, New Jersey

DRILLS TO PERFECT SHOOTING

Jack Rodgers has coached basketball at Harrison High School for six years. His first two years were as an assistant with a total record of 39-4, including a 19-game winning streak (1971:20-2; 1972:19-2) and two conference championships. 1973 was his first varsity season. Harrison finished with an 18-6 record. They were 11-1 in conference play and won the first varsity conference title in the school's history. His combined record is 86-51 with three conference championships.

Good shooting is no accident, nor is it something to be left to chance. Many coaches take to the theory that a player will always practice his shooting on his own. The reason for this is that, other than dribbling, there aren't too many other fundamentals a player can practice alone.

Note: This is true. But as with other skills, he may be practicing incorrectly, thereby forming bad habits or constantly experimenting with his shot and never gaining confidence.

For example, many ball players cannot shoot without first bouncing the ball. Regardless of how talented the boy is, one extra bounce against a good defensive player can result in your so-called "good shooter" eating the ball. This common fault develops from the player practicing his shooting alone—and is one of the many reasons why we employ drills to perfect shooting.

IT WORKS

During the past season, our team shot 55% from the floor and 82% from the foul line. This was a team with one player taller than six feet, including a player five feet six inches who shot 55% from the field. The starting team was composed of four juniors who never played in varsity competition and a senior. They averaged 78 points per game, while winning the conference championship. This was no accident—our drill program works.

DRILL PROGRAM

During practice each boy will take at least 150 shots from the field. This includes layups and jump shots. He will shoot at least 100 fouls. All this shooting is incorporated into drills and is supervised.

Note: You may think that this takes a lot of time—but it doesn't. The total time spent is but one-half hour spread out through the individual practice session. The added benefit is that these drills, like so many, incorporate more than one skill, plus they serve as conditioners. Our players are taught the fundamentals of good shooting throughout our program using these drills—so it becomes a matter of proficiency and confidence when they reach the varsity level.

FULL-COURT THREE MAN UP AND DOWN

The first drill we use is a variation on the full-court three man up and down. After we have done our layups in this manner we change it to a jump shot drill. The coach stations himself at mid-court as the three players go down the floor. (See Diagram 1.)

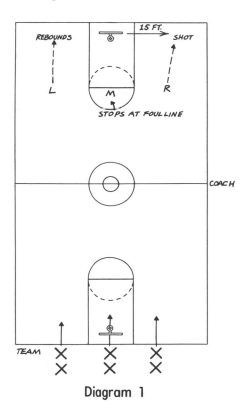

Diagram 1

Note: At no time does the ball touch the floor—we insist on this. We have found that the less dribbling we do and the more passing, the greater number of open shots we get.

As the players approach the foul line, the coach calls "middle," "left" or "right." The player, upon receiving the pass, takes a jump shot without walking or bouncing the ball. As in a fast break, which this drill simulates, the middle man stops at the foul line, but unlike in the fast break, the wings, instead of cutting, stay about 15 feet from the hoop. The ball is rebounded by the opposite wing. The lanes are filled and they return to the other basket, where the procedure is repeated. Then the next group of three players goes.

Note: In this drill, as in all the drills, we emphasize passing. The pass is just as important as the shot. If the pass is not thrown or caught properly, you might as well have bounced the ball—because the good open shot will no longer be there. With a team as small as ours, the quicker we take advantage of the open shot the better.

SPEED SHOOTING DRILL

In this drill, we incorporate speed with our foul shooting. Two players pair up at each of our six baskets. After they complete their fouls, the drill begins. (See Diagram 2.)

Note: We shoot fouls throughout practice in groups of 30, 20, 20, 20, 10. The last ten are for team competition. To simulate game conditions, the fouls are shot after strenuous drills for a fatigue factor. The players shoot two fouls at a time and exchange positions.

The drill begins with P (passer) under the basket and S (shooter) from the spot in the diagram marked "X-15ft." P passes to S, who shoots without bouncing the ball. S does not move until P rebounds the ball—then he head fakes, jab steps, etc., and breaks for the next spot.

Once again, the pass is emphasized. S shoots the jumper immediately. When S has the shot from all the spots he reverses his direction and repeats the procedure—then the players exchange positions.

HALF-COURT THREE MAN WEAVE LAYUP

The final drill is used at the end of practice—and we also use it as a warm-up drill. It is a half-court drill, a variation of the three man weave layup. (See Diagram 3.)

Note: We use this drill in warm-ups because it serves that exact purpose. It warms up the players. I have found by watching pre-game warm-ups that too much time is spent by players just shooting wherever they want, standing around, and in general doing what they won't be doing in a game. During this time, they are also cooling off. This drill employs

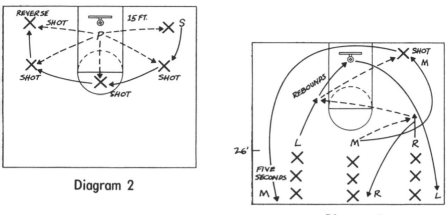

Diagram 2

Diagram 3

things we will use in a game—plus it gets the players physically ready.

We start with three lines at approximately the 26-foot line. The ball starts in the middle. The middle man passes to the right and cuts behind the man he passes to. Player R passes to player L and goes to the middle line. Player L passes to player M and continues to the boards for the rebound. M, instead of going for a layup lazily, stays about 15 feet out and takes a short jumper. L rebounds, returns to line R. M goes to line L.

Upon a signal from the coach or player, the procedure is reversed with the pass going to the left side, then finally with the shooter faking to one side and taking a jumper from the foul line. We have a 12-man squad and try to keep three balls going at once. This keeps the players involved and forces them to concentrate—which is the mark of a good shooter. Once again, the ball never hits the floor except for a bounce pass.

Note: These drills have been very successful for us, as our statistics show. Repetition breeds skill. Skill brings success. Repeated success creates confidence. And every coach knows what confidence brings—more success. Confidence, that's the key.

CONCLUSION

Let me cite one instance. In a game last season, there were ten seconds left on the clock—and we were behind by one point with possession of the ball.

Believe me, it's a nice problem to have five men in a huddle who know they can sink the ball—and seven others on the bench with the same feeling about themselves.

To have 12 players who believe that if they have the last shot they will win—is one of the fruits derived from practicing shooting. Because good shooting is no accident.

By the way, we won the game.

3   Robert L. Metcalf

Director of Athletics
University High School
Normal, Illinois

SHOOTING DRILLS: THEORIES AND PRACTICES

Robert L. Metcalf has coached Illinois High School Basketball teams to twenty-nine championships, including eight regional and three sectional titles in twenty-four years of high school coaching in the state. After four years at Waterman, he served as basketball coach at Glenbard West, Glen Ellyn, for seven years and is now in his fourteenth year as head basketball coach at University High School. His overall record is 395 wins against 233 losses. Coach Metcalf completed requirements for a doctor of physical education at Indiana University in 1970 and has served in the past as president of IHSCA.

The following theories and practices of basketball shooting are based on twenty years of playing the game and twenty-two years of coaching it. It is obvious that the theories of basketball shooting are almost as numerous as the coaches in the game.

Note: They go from one extreme to the other—where all the shooting is "free" shooting or unsupervised, to the very strict control of every minute of shooting practice.

29

As I see it, basketball shooting drills should incorporate the following basic principles:

1. Drills should simulate game conditions.
2. Shots should be taken from those areas where play-ers are most likely to shoot during a game.
3. Drills should be run at a fairly fast pace.
4. Drills should be varied, interesting and competitive.

DAILY DRILLS

The following three drills can be used almost daily and permit excellent shooting practice, as well as the opportunity for instruction and coaching.

● *Quick shooting drill:* For this drill, one boy rebounds and another boy shoots from the position at which he is most likely to shoot during a regular game. The player shooting moves from one position to another and the ball is returned to him quickly for his shots.

> Note: He may dribble the ball and occasionally drive. This is a snappy drill. The players change from shooter to rebounder every two minutes. We usually run this drill for about ten minutes.

While this drill is being executed, the centers usually are working at a side basket. Centers work with a defensive man on them—all of the time. We feed the centers the ball from the various offensive positions.

● *Break down shooting drill:* We use this almost daily dur-ing the pre-season practice. This type of drill is based on the offenses normally used—so that the player is actually practic-ing each shot from the position he plays in that offense. He takes the shot with a pass or dribble as it would happen in a game. Fakes and preliminary moves usually executed by the player are made before taking the shot. Following is an ex-ample of the drill from a 1-3-1 offense.

> Example: The wing man reverses from the wing position and cuts for the basket. The pass is made either by the point man

in the offense or the high post man. The extra wing men fill all
the lanes so that the passes are made from the high post and
the point positions.

This is an excellent drill for the coach to observe faulty
mechanics such as failure to fake properly, stop properly, or
move properly. We also check for shooting off balance,
jumping forward on the jump shot, and other errors of this
nature.

Note: During this shooting drill, we do not stress one-on-one
basketball play for the offensive man. We develop this
through a variety of one-on-one defensive drills that we employ throughout the year.

• *Two-line shooting drill:* For this drill we form two lines
at each end of the floor, with three or four boys in a line.
They go for the basket and work on layups and short jump
shots. We do not want the boys to make any moves—just go
in and make the basket.

Note: For the layup stage of the drill, we place a coach or
manager under the basket who is a good faker. He bumps the
shooter as he comes in for the layup. For the jump shot stage
of the drill, we stress stopping and making the short jump.

We start the drill by taking three or four turns from the
same line, then changing ends—which means that those who
are going in on the right side of the basket will now be going
in on the left side when they change ends. We go for three or
four minutes and change ends again.

Note: If there is some particular move you want the boys to
master, you add that to the drill—change of pace dribble,
driving in for the reverse layup, etc.

During all shooting drills, the coach should be on the
floor, observing. It's the time for instruction. Also, a great
many times we incorporate a half-defense into the drills—the
defensive man plays a good, tough defense and can do anything defensively but block the shot.

PRE-GAME NIGHT SHOOTING DRILLS

These are the drills at which our players seem to work the hardest. We've been doing some variation of the following drills for the past fifteen years.

• *When:* We execute these drills before a game—thus, for a Friday night game, we drill on Thursday afternoon; for a Tuesday night game, we drill on Monday afternoon.

• *Squad division:* The squad is divided into teams of three members each. It is best if each team has a basket to themselves. Four on a team can be used but it is not as satisfactory.

• *Floor position:* All of the shooting is done from 9, 15 and 21 feet from the basket at one of five positions at these distances. That is, straight out from the basket; straight out to each side; and at two positions equidistant between these (or 45° angle from the basket).

Note: The five positions are marked in Diagram 1 at each of the distances. Since the entire squad is involved in these drills we shoot mostly from 9 and 15 feet. We do very little shooting from 21 feet.

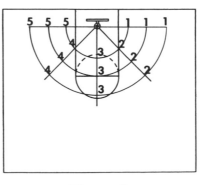

Diagram 1

• *Objectives:* The drills are designed to force the player to shoot quickly, maintain a high level of accuracy, hustle to rebound his own shot (except from 21 feet), and build endurance.

● *Conditions of play:* The drills are timed to see: (1) how many baskets can be made in a specific time, say 20 or 30 seconds; (2) a specific number of consecutive baskets made; (3) which team makes a specific number of baskets first.

DRILL EXAMPLES

● *Layups:* We usually start the drills right under the basket, shooting the jump layup from the left or right side. We go for a specific number and it is usually the first team to make 25. In this drill, if you miss once you usually don't win.

Note: The premium, of course, is to hustle. You are close to the basket and seldom miss. But it's a good way to get the boys started for the remainder of the drills.

● *Nine-foot shots:* At the 9-foot distance you have to change the rules frequently. If you shoot for a specific number all of the time, the boys slow down too much. If you shoot for a consecutive number, they again have a tendency to go a little too slow to simulate game conditions. So we put a premium on accuracy and speed by using the following scoring system.

Shoot for 20 seconds. The team that makes the most field goals will get one point and the team that took the most shots will get one point. However, if the team that took the most shots also made the most field goals, they get an additional point—or total of three points. With this system, no points are awarded unless a team makes half of the shots attempted.

Note: A simple way to total shots and baskets is to have one boy record the number of shots taken and another boy record the number of shots made. For example, a team making 7 out of 15 shots cannot win.

Shooting for consecutive field goals really puts pressure on the players, especially if the players are good shooters or

are hitting. Normally, at nine feet, we have them shoot for a
string of at least twice the number of team players plus one.
For example, if three players are on each shooting team, we
have them make six or seven in a row.

> Note: There is a lot of pressure put on the fifth, sixth and
> seventh shots—and if there is a miss, of course, they start
> over again.

● *Fifteen-foot shots:* At the 15-foot distance, we normally
have them shoot to make one more than the number of
players on the squad. So if there are three boys on a team
they must make four shots. The boy who makes the first shot
of a string is going to have to put in the last one for his team
to win.

If they are hitting exceptionally well you can go up to
five or six, but you do not want the games to run overly long.
Each team keeps a record of the number of points they score
during the drills. We finish this series of shooting drills with
free-throw shooting.

● *Free-throws:* Each team shoots free-throws one at a
time for a total of ten free-throws. Therefore, if there are
three boys on each team, they each shoot three free-throws
one at a time and the best shooter on a team shoots four so
that ten free-throws are attempted.

> Note: We place one player from each team at a basket so
> there is some team competition. Other players can razz the
> free-throw shooter, or do anything to distract them as long as
> they do not make any free-throw lane violations by getting
> into the lane too soon.

At this point in the drill the coach can put as much stress
on the free-throw shooting as he desires. For example, let's
say that during the practice, team A has 16 points; team B
has 14 points; team C has 10 points. To make the free-throw
phase of the drills more competitive, the coach can let each
free-throw be worth more than one point.

> Example: Chances are that no team is going to make less than
> five out of ten—so you have five points which will determine

the winning team. Say that the shots are worth five points each. For the team with 16 points to be sure of winning, they must make at least one more free throw than team B or two more than team C. If team C makes ten out of ten, and team A makes eight, and team B nine—team A would have 56 points while team B would have 59 points and team C would come out with 50 plus 10 points for a total of 60, which makes them the winner. If the teams have been very even in the field goal shooting, and only one or two points separate the top from the bottom, you can make each free-throw worth just one point. (See Chart I.)

Chart I: Team Scores					
	Team A		**Team B**		**Team C**
Points FG Shooting	16		14		10
Points FT Shooting (8 × 5)	40	(9 × 5)	45	(10 × 5)	50
Totals	56		59		60

CONCLUSION

While some of this sounds detailed and time-consuming, it really isn't. Once the boys get involved in the competition, they really work at their shooting. I can say from experience that these shooting theories and practices have improved our game.

4   Gene Snell

Junior Varsity Basketball Coach
Dearborn High School
Dearborn, Michigan

PRESSURE FREE-THROW DRILLS

As junior varsity basketball coach at Dearborn High School, Gene Snell has a six-year record of 81 wins against 33 losses for a .710 percentage. He has never had a losing season. His league play record is 62 wins against 14 losses.

Basketball coaches agree that successful free-throw shooting is essential for success during the season. Free-throw accuracy is especially helpful late in a game, when things may get hectic. The ability to make free throws under pressure can help turn a game around, or enable a team to insure its victory.

Because of the importance of free throws, our team uses a variety of free-throw drills that create pressure and competition. We attempt to make the free throw second nature to our players—as much a part of their game as the layup.

Three of our most important drills are the Free Throw Ladder, One and One, and Seventy Percent. These drills have improved the free-throw accuracy of our players, and they should help improve the shooting skill of your players, too.

Free-Throw Rule: Although I try to help poor free-throw shooters by teaching specific stance, hand position, posture and follow-through, the important principle is to *do it the same way every time.* Once a player discovers a fairly successful style, consistency is what counts—even under the most adverse conditions.

FREE THROW LADDER

We use the Free Throw Ladder every day, and it serves more than one purpose. The Ladder, itself, is a Masonite pegboard with a sturdy frame. The name of each player, written on white poster paper, is hung on the pegboard.

At the outset of each season, the players pair off and shoot 25 free throws each. The player with the best total out of 25 is placed at the top position on the Ladder. The player with the second best total is placed at the second position, and so on. If there are ties, the players involved shoot one shot at a time in overtime, until a winner is determined.

Each day, thereafter, the players challenge one another in an even-odd pattern. One day Number Two challenges Number One, Number Four challenges Number Three, Number Six challenges Number Five, and so on.

If we have an odd number of team members, the last player has no challenge that day. The next day, the Odds challenge the Evens: Number Three challenges Number Two, Number Five challenges Number Four, and so on. On this day, the Number One shooter has no challenge. The first or last players, if they have no challenge, shoot 25 free throws alone.

In the challenge, each player shoots 25 free throws at a time, alternating with his opponent. The player with the most shots made out of 25 is the winner. Again, if they tie, they shoot one shot at a time in overtime until a winner is determined. The winner adjusts his name on the Ladder if he has moved up.

● *Value of drill:* This drill is especially valuable in that it helps the players develop foul-shooting consistency. It is also a highly competitive drill. A player may move up a step every day if he continues to win, and everyone can see his progress.

Note: The Ladder also determines who will shoot technical fouls during games. If a technical is called during a game, the player on the top of the Ladder at that time shoots the resulting free throw. This makes the Ladder even more valuable to the squad.

ONE AND ONE

Another drill we use regularly is One and One. In this drill the players split into groups of two or three at a basket and shoot free throws, one and one. If they make the first shot, they shoot a second before the next player shoots. If they miss the first shot, the next player takes his position at the line and shoots, one and one.

At irregular intervals I blow the whistle and all activity stops. I call out the name of a player standing at the line, and he must shoot one shot while all the other players look on. The silence is frightening.

If the player makes the free throw, the drill continues as before (after loud cheers and applause). If he misses, all players must sprint two laps (good-naturedly chiding the shooter for choking) before resuming the drill. This is a fun drill, and it keeps the players loose at the line.

• *Value of drill:* The drill creates pressure, and a competitive situation. Each player must make his first shot to get his second. And he must make his "solo" free throw while all eyes are watching. He is under further pressure because he and his teammates must run if he misses. As the drill progresses, the players must shoot while slightly winded, a game condition.

SEVENTY PERCENT

Perhaps the most demanding of our free-throw drills is Seventy Percent. I use this drill periodically at the end of practice as a conditioner and a free-throw drill.

Players count off by two's; then they all "run the lines," as we call it. Starting along the baseline, the squad sprints to the free-throw line and back, then to the mid-court line and back, then to the far free-throw line and back, and finally to the opposite baseline and back.

When they complete the sprints, Group One steps out, and each member shoots one free throw in his turn while Group Two watches. Then Group One returns to the baseline and the team "runs the lines" again. This time when they finish the sprints, Group Two steps out and shoots a free throw each. This process is repeated so that each group goes to the line twice between intervals of sprints:

1. All players run the lines.
2. Group one shoots a free throw each.
3. All players run the lines.
4. Group two shoots a free throw each.
5. All players run the lines.
6. Group one again shoots a free throw each.
7. All players run the lines.
8. Group two again shoots a free throw each.

As the players shoot, I keep track of how many shots are made. At the end of the drill the squad must have completed 70 percent of its free throws in order to "shower-up." For instance, a team of ten players shoots 20 foul shots (two each) during the drill. At the end of that drill, the team must have made 14 out of 20 shots, or 70 percent. If they don't shoot 70 percent, they run the drill again, this time cutting off one shot from 70 percent (instead of 14 of 20, they must make 13 of 20). If they continue to fall short of the mark, they cut off one shot each time, but never go below 50 percent (i.e., 10 of 20). If they reach the 50 percent mark, they start at the 70 percent again.

This drill may last as long as 20 to 30 minutes early in the season; so we give ourselves plenty of time to run it. But by mid-season, Seventy Percent rarely lasts more than two or three sets. In fact, the past three times I have used the drill this year, the team has completed 70 percent in the first set.

Note: If the drill starts to go on for too long, we institute a "bonus" situation. If a group can make all of its shots (i.e., five of five), we call it a practice.

• *Value of drill:* This drill creates a pressure situation and is competitive. Each player must do his part; so it is a good team drill. It is also a tremendous drill for developing consistency under adverse conditions. The players are fatigued, alone at the line, and know that if they make their shots, they can go; if they don't, more sprints. It demands tremendous concentration.

As we get more proficient at the line, the players tease each other, make faces, yell, and do anything they can think of to create distractions for the shooters. They honestly feel they can make the shot no matter what the pressure.

This is the aim of our drills. We try to block all things out of our minds except for the basket, the ball, and the mechanics of the shot. We use several other free-throw drills for variety and to avoid stale practices, but these three drills are basic and can give rise to new variations of other drills.

TEAM SUCCESS

On the junior-varsity team, made up predominantly of sophomores, our free-throw shooting percentage has always been at or above the 60 percent mark. This may not seem high, but it is for the age of our players and their level of play. This is a season mark however, and it doesn't represent our free-throw proficiency when in pressure situations.

For instance, this year while behind at the end of the third quarter by nine points, we won the game by virtue of making 13 of 14 free throws in the fourth quarter. And in another game, we came from behind in the fourth quarter to win on the strength of making eight of eight free throws. Also, while holding on to leads late in the game, we have increased our leads by capitalizing on fouls made by the opposition trying to gain control of the ball. I feel that the three drills I've discussed have directly resulted in our success under pressure in many ball games.

5

Charles A. Field

Assistant Basketball Coach
Towson State College
Baltimore, Maryland

DRILLS FOR TEACHING REBOUNDING

Charles Field, Jr. has been coaching in the high school and college ranks since 1959. He has coached football, basketball, and baseball at the following schools: St. Leo Prep (Belmont, N.C.) Military School; St. Mary's (Annapolis, Md.) High School; Annapolis (Md.) High School; Anne Arundel (Severna Park, Md.) Junior College. At present, he's an assistant coach in basketball and baseball, director of intramurals, and assistant professor in Physical Education at Towson State College.

One of the most important phases of basketball is rebounding. Many coaches feel it's 75% of the game. Adolph Rupp stated, "He who controls the back boards controls the game."

Each time you fail to get the rebound after a shot attempt, it gives your opponents another opportunity to score. With the majority of teams shooting 40 and 50% from the field, you just can't allow a team too many second and third shots without giving up two points practically every time they come down the court with the ball.

Note: Whether you're a fast-breaking team, as we are, or a slow, deliberate, ball-control team, the coach should spend a great majority of time on individual and team rebounding techniques. Since so many games are won or lost on the boards, it's essential that the boys become aware of the importance of this phase of basketball. Rebounding is an important fundamental that is sometimes considered necessary only for the tall players—but any boy can improve his rebounding ability by practice and effort.

PHILOSOPHY

Some players have an intuitive sense, or a special basketball know-how, which enables them to get to the right spot at the right time. If these players are tall, strong and well-coordinated, they can handle their team's rebounding responsibilities almost single-handed. But no coach can rely on just one rebounder. Every player on the team must be taught this great asset and take pride in getting his share of the team's rebounds.

At Towson State College we must stress rebounding and encourage an aggressive, clean type of toughness on the boards because most of our opponents are bigger. During the past three seasons we had only one 6'5" boy. This past season our center was 6'4" and the other starters were not over 6'2". Pretty small for college, you'd agree, but we've had good winning teams that have gone to the conference tournament each year.

Note: We strongly believe that rebounding and winning go hand in hand, and work at this aspect of the game daily. We always praise strong board work and find little use for the player who does not like to rebound and play the game with pride. There is little doubt that the "law of averages" will defeat a team that cannot rebound.

REBOUNDING DRILLS

While there is no easy way to teach rebounding to young players at any level—we employ a number of drills that we feel accomplish our aims most effectively.

TIP: To help in this respect we try to sell our team and our rebounders on one idea: Superior rebounding is a necessity—when anyone on the team shoots, the rebounders must go to the board.

• *High jump drill:* We set up as shown in Diagram 1. Players jump back and forth over a bar a specified number of times. Raise or lower the bar as needed. Do not run; jump from standing position.

Note: To aid in jumping also employ the "donkey drill"—whereby a boy does 25 toe raises with another player on his back.

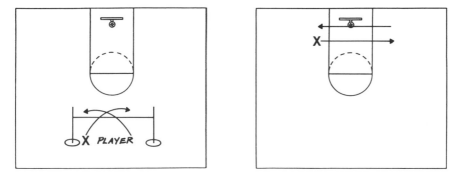

Diagram 1   Diagram 2

• *Superman drill:* For this drill (Diagram 2), we stand outside of the lane and throw the ball against the board on the other side and rebound outside the lane. Go back and forth landing with a good base.

• *Release drill:* One player throws the ball up (Diagram 3); a second player rebounds aggressively; the first player checks the rebounder's technique and fundamentals. As the player rebounds, he makes a half turn in the air and passes the ball swiftly.

• *Anticipation drill:* With rebounder or tipping ring in the basket, each player goes where the ball is likely to hit —only after the ball has hit the rebound ring (Diagram 4). He faces the basket and goes to the end of the line after his turn.

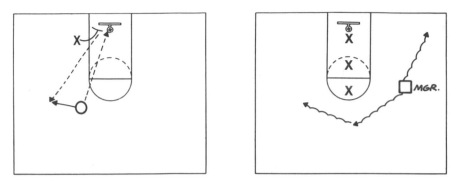

Diagram 3   Diagram 4

Note: A manager can direct the drill. Move players farther out after a time. With hustle and determination they can rebound over 70% before the ball hits the floor.

● *Free-for-all drill:* Coach or manager throws ball up and the three players attempt to rebound (Diagram 5). The player getting the ball must go right back up with it. The other two players use considerable body contact to hinder the rebounder's attempted shot.

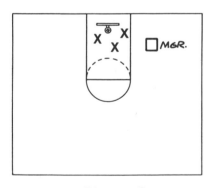

Diagram 5

Tip: The players are not allowed to get outside the lane. Add two more players if desirable. This instills toughness and aggressiveness.

• *Burst out drill:* For this drill, offensive player 01 shoots; X1 rebounds and fights through the double team by bursting out (Diagram 6) very low with the body—and then dribbling.

• *Baseline drill:* Three defensive players attempt to beat three offensive players (Diagram 7) with aggressive boxing out, maintaining contact and rebounding properly. A manager can direct the drill.

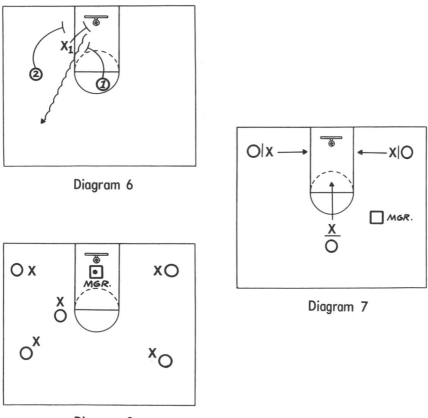

Diagram 6

Diagram 7

Diagram 8

• *Team scramble drill:* A manager places the ball on the floor (Diagram 8) as the defensive players make contact, hold contact and keep their men away from the ball for three to five seconds.

REBOUNDING TIPS

1. Probably 80% of high school players jump flat-footed and never push off their toes. Jumping from the toes adds at least three inches if the arms are fully extended. Jumping flat-footed must be corrected.

2. Stress the following fundamentals in each drill or workout: flexibility in the knees; elbows out to the side; fingers spread and pointed upwards; eyes focused on the rim (most important).

3. Always land in a good body balance without spreading out those legs too much. Otherwise you can never get a good quick pass out or pivot away from pressure.

4. Anticipation is a key on missed shots. Expect every shot to be missed and always observe the angle from where the shot was taken. Study the arc. A high arc will bounce high and a hard shot will bounce out.

> **Tip:** Knowing what type of shot your opponent shoots and from what position on the court will help.

5. Never get stuck underneath the hoop. Always readjust your position if your defensive man has the better position. If you just move to the middle of the court, you are taking his better position away from him. He may even lose you—so always move around and keep him busy.

6. Blocking out should be used in competitive drills every day. From your defensive position, master the art of boxing out with a reverse pivot. In this method you cover more area and get more body contact into your opponent. Watch out for his attempt to reverse pivot and spin off you.

> **Tip:** This reverse pivot is an effective offensive move and tough to counter—but be ready to shuffle your feet and slide with him.

7. Make a half turn in the air always—unless you're being double-teamed. If you're being double-teamed, you must bring the ball very low to the ground and break out of there between the two men.

8. Getting rid of the ball quickly and surely will keep the defense "off your back," and as a result rebounding will be much easier. Make that outlet pass to the same side right away and use the dribble only as a last resort or a safety valve.

9. Second effort is imperative in rebounding. On the offensive board a good second effort keeps the ball in play and results in many two pointers. On the defensive board, great effort limits the opposition to one shot. Be very aggressive.

10. Constantly build your legs through ropes, jumping benches, running stairs, repeated leaping, and the like.

FIVE-POINT SUMMARY

1. Rebounding is most important to continued success.

2. There is no easy method or short cut for mastering the techniques of rebounding. It must be emphasized and practiced competitively very often. Contact drills are necessary to develop aggressiveness.

3. Be determined—give a great second-effort with all-out hustle and go get the ball.

4. Anticipation is important to rebounding—and each player must assume the responsibility of rebounding.

5. Rules, aids and drills all help in improving each player's rebounding ability.

6

Chic Hess

Head Basketball Coach
Loyalsock Township High School
Williamsport, Pennsylvania

ALL-PURPOSE DRIBBLING DRILL

Charles J. Hess has been coaching high school basketball for eight years. His coaching career began at Medill Bair (Fairless Hills, Pennsylvania) High School where his teams compiled a 38-12 mark. At present, Coach Hess is at Loyalsock High School where his teams have compiled a 61-32 record. His overall mark is 99-44. Coach Hess is also Director of the Lebanon (Pennsylvania) Basketball Camp.

One of the most important fundamentals of basketball is the art of dribbling. Good ball handling develops confidence, and confident players are necessary for winning basketball games.

Note: Many players find dribbling an enjoyable skill to perform. Oftentimes, they are guilty of dribbling too much.

Of all the fundamental skills in the game, dribbling is perhaps the easiest to master. Because of the nature of the skill, a player doesn't have to possess exceptional physical ability such as stamina, speed, and strength to excel as a dribbler. Since it's so important and easy to teach, coaches should spend more time teaching and reviewing the different types of dribbles.

Note: Like all basketball skills, dribbling must be learned and
continuously reviewed in practice. The elementary and
junior-high-school programs provide excellent opportunities
to introduce students to the fundamental skills of dribbling.

DRIBBLING

First, players must be taught how to dribble:

- Move on the balls of the feet.
- Keep knees slightly bent.
- Push the ball with the fingertips and use slight wrist
  movement.
- Bend the body from the waist.
- Keep the head up to see an open man or shot.
- Keep the body between the opponent and the ball.

The player should also know when to dribble:

- When driving for the basket.
- When closely guarded.
- When setting a screen.
- When advancing the ball across mid-court.
- When freezing the ball or spreading the offense to set
  up a play.

After these rudiments have been established, you may
have your players master the basic dribbles. Some of the basic
dribbles that we feel are important have been incorporated
into one all-purpose drill. This drill, when all aspects of it
have been introduced, takes no more than six minutes to
complete.

We feel that this six-minute drill, which we run at the
beginning of each practice, has greatly helped our offense by
reducing our number of turnovers per game. Following are
the dribble moves that we concentrate on.

DRIBBLE MOVES

- *Fingertip control:* Give each player his own ball. Have
the player stay within a circular area, diameter approxi-

mately five yards long. The player should practice dribbling with either hand. He should dribble the ball low, between his legs, and behind his back.

• *Whirl dribble:* The whirl dribble is very advantageous to the offensive player who has started his drive and has been cut off by a defensive player. The dribbler pulls the ball back with his dribbling hand. This prevents him from palming. He spins, with his back to the defender, and moves toward the basket. The player shoots with his opposite hand.

> Note: If necessary, this dribble can be used out front to avoid the defensive man. The offensive man uses the whirl movement and then continues to dribble.

• *Behind-the-back dribble:* The player who has good wrists and good ball control can attempt this move. It's usually attempted out front when the defense overplays the dribbler to the side he's dribbling on. This close defense causes the dribbler to flip the ball behind his back, letting it hit the floor. The player then continues to dribble.

• *Crossover dribble:* This dribble is attempted when a defensive man is overplaying the offensive man to the side he's dribbling. The dribbler pushes the ball to his opposite hand immediately before reaching the defensive player.

> Note: This move is mostly out front on a fast break, but it can be used in close to drive by the defensive man.

• *Hockey dribble:* The dribbler moves close to the defensive player, dribbling quickly and low. The dribbler fakes with his head and shoulders continuously just before making his move to go by the man. This dribble is begun with either hand, but the dribbler should switch hands when he makes his move past the defender.

• *Hesitation dribble:* This dribble is used to throw the defense off stride. A player who is dribbling may change the speed of his dribble, depending on his plan to shake off the defense. He may come to a complete stop while continuing his dribble and then quickly change his pace, continuing on.

LINE DRIBBLING DRILL

Our dribbling drill uses the lines on a regulation court to give direction to the players. Following the lines of the court, the players find designated spots where they are to execute different dribbles.

The drill begins with all players positioned along the baseline with a ball. The players are spaced evenly, and they face the court. In this position, indicated as position 1, the players do the fingertip-control dribble until the coach signals the first player to start down the lines of the court (Diagram 1). At each designated position, indicated as position 2, the players execute the whirl dribble.

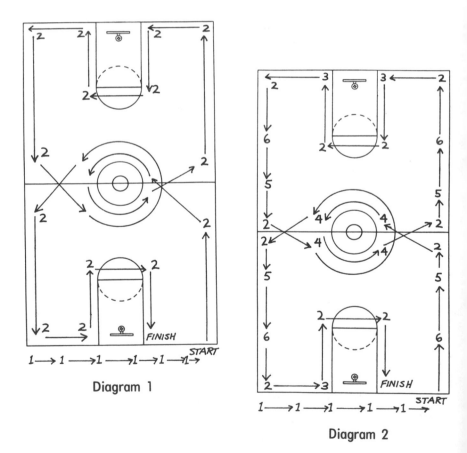

Diagram 1

Diagram 2

Note: All the players will continue around the court until each one has traced all the lines and returned to the starting position. At the center circle, all players will go to the right, regardless of the side from which they are approaching.

After the players have familiarized themselves with the procedure, other dribbling skills can be added to the drill at designated spots (indicated as position 3, position 4, and so on). See Diagram 2.

To further the challenge, dark glasses (dribbling aids) should be used. These glasses, if used correctly, will prevent the players from watching the ball while dribbling. These glasses will not only help keep players interested—they'll produce great player improvement.

Note: The left hand can be developed by switching the starting position of the All-Purpose Drill. When the starting position is reversed, the dribbling procedure is reversed.

No coach will doubt that improved dribbling skills can only help improve his team's performance. The All-Purpose Drill, used regularly with the dark glasses, will produce a noticeable improvement in all players. This drill can also be altered to incorporate other dribbling skills such as between-the-legs dribbling and so on. All the coach needs to do is specify the dribbling skill he would like performed at a designated spot along the court lines.

Former Head Basketball Coach
Valparaiso High School
Valparaiso, Indiana

DRIBBLING DRILLS WITH
THE "DRIBBLE AID"

Virgil Sweet was head basketball coach at Valparaiso High School for twenty years, during which time his teams won fourteen sectional championships. Previously, Valparaiso had won only one sectional trophy in twenty-three years. His invention, the "Dribble Aid," has been widely accepted by the coaching profession and is largely responsible for the success of his boys who went on to play college ball. Now retired from active coaching, Virgil Sweet is Executive Director of the Indiana Basketball Coaches Association.

A trend toward more dribbling in offensive basketball has begun and will be on the increase in coming years. This may be because pressing defenses close all passing lanes and play for the interception; or perhaps it is simply that forwards and centers are able to dribble in a manner once reserved for guards. Whatever the reason, it is evident that the coach who expects to win is going to have to develop good dribblers at all positions.

DRIBBLE AID

Dribbling drills are a part of our daily practice sessions. We have found that even our best dribblers watch the ball—without realizing it—as they dribble. To combat this, we always use *dribble aids* in our dribbling drills and when we play one-on-one. The dribble aid is a flexible plastic device with an elastic headband that permits the dribbler to see in front of him but hides the ball from his vision.

Drills for teaching dribbling that we have found to be most effective are explained below. Any number of players may take part in the drills; each boy has a dribble aid and a ball.

- *Survival drill:* Each player, with a ball and a dribble aid, must continue dribbling within boundary lanes at all times. The object is for each player to try to bat the ball away from another player. When a participant has his ball knocked away or if he loses control while attempting to hit another player's ball, he is out of the game. Last player to "survive" is the winner.
- *Dribble tag:* Players are restricted to a certain area, depending on the number of participants. Two players are designated as "it" and must keep one hand up until they tag another player, who then raises his hand so everyone knows whom to avoid. Any player losing control of the ball while attempting to make a tag is still "it." The drill runs continuously without eliminating anyone.
- *Figure eight drill:* This drill is most effective with a large number of players participating. Half of the players line up side by side on the end line, between the free-throw lane and the sideline, facing downcourt. The other half line up on the same end line, on the other side of the lane.

Each group is instructed to dribble a figure eight around the three circles on the court. All players start simultaneously and the two groups will meet between the free-throw circle and the center circle. As the drill continues, the two groups will be going in opposite directions and will continually meet each other.

NOT A RACE

The drill should not be a race, but the players should stop, back up, move laterally, and use a change of pace as they thread their way through the other players.

The dribbler should always dribble with the hand away from the circle. With experienced dribblers, a man may be placed in each of the three circles and permitted to deflect the ball from any player who dribbles with the incorrect hand.

There is no elimination or competition in this drill: the purpose of the drill is mobility, not speed.

In addition to the drills described above, we have isolated the dribble moves that occur most frequently in our offensive attack; at the beginning of each practice the players execute these "twelve basic dribbles" while wearing dribble aids. The idea is presented here so that each coach can select the basic dribble moves which best fit his system. The important thing is that players execute isolated dribble drills every day.

The trend back toward more dribbling has started and the "thinking coach" should prepare his team for competition in the basketball of tomorrow.

8

Mike Tramuta

Assistant Basketball Coach
Fredonia State College
Fredonia, New York

A DRIBBLING AND BALL-HANDLING SERIES

Mike Tramuta coached high school basketball for eleven years, the last few at Dunkirk (New York) High School, and compiled an overall record of 102 wins against 61 losses. At present, he is assistant basketball coach at Fredonia State College.

We collected the following series of drills over the years to help youngsters develop hands for both dribbling and quickness in general. They provide boys at the high school level with an instructional yet fun program for improving their ball handling.

Note: We use these drills with all our players—both big and little men. We feel that a youngster can learn to become a good ball handler and develop quick hands if he will just work at it. These drills are performed every day for at least 15 minutes in an organized session.

DRIBBLE SERIES

Phase 1: Ball does not touch the floor.

- *Tipping:* Hold ball over head with elbows extended;

up as high as possible on the toes. Tip ball back and forth on fingertips. You may look at the ball.

• *Funnel:* Same starting position as tipping; keeping ball always at arm's length with elbows extended, continue to tip ball while bringing it down in front of body to floor and back over head. Bend knees to get ball to floor.

• *Circle neck:* Bring ball around neck changing hands in rear of neck; continue in circle and then reverse circle.

• *Circle body:* Bring ball around body changing hands in rear of body; continue in circle and then reverse circle. Keep head up.

• *Circle legs:* Bring feet together; bend knees and carry ball around bent legs in circle; reverse circle. It is important to keep head up.

• *Leg circles (left and right):* Stride stance; bring ball around forward leg and reverse. Do the same drill with the opposite leg forward. Keep head up.

• *Figure-8:* Parallel stance; do not move feet; bring ball in and out of legs in figure eight fashion; then reverse figure eight. Keep head up.

• *Cradle:* Parallel stance; ball is held between legs with one hand in front and the other in rear. Objective is to move hands to reverse position while ball remains between legs.

• *Tunnel:* Parallel stance; bend over at waist with ball held at arms' length. Objective is to bring ball through legs and catch behind legs. Then toss ball forward through legs and catch with arms extended.

• *Forward march:* Walk forward; bring ball in and out of legs. Important to bring ball from inside to outside so that feet do not come too high off floor. Look at ball when learning, then do drill with head up.

• *Ball slam:* Erect stance; hold ball above head with right hand. Left hand is kept at side with palm up; slam ball into left hand by bringing ball down fast from above head. Do not move left hand towards ball. Reverse procedure.

Phase 2: Dribble with one basketball.

• *Dribble around leg:* Stride stance with right leg forward. Place left hand behind back; with right hand, dribble ball around right leg in circle; reverse circle. Look at ball when learning. Do same drill with left leg forward.

• *Dribbling 8's:* Similar to figure eight drill without touching floor; only now dribble ball. Reverse the figure eight after a short time.

• *Dribbling circle:* Bring legs and feet together; bend knees slightly and dribble ball in circle around legs. Then reverse circle. You can look at ball while learning.

• *Bridge:* Kneel with stride stance; dribble ball back and forth under forward bent knee; then dribble around foot and under knee. Next dribble completely around body while kneeling. Reverse position and do the same set.

• *Whirl:* Sit down with knees up; dribble a ball completely around body. Reverse dribble.

• *Under and over:* Sit down with legs extended. Begin with right-hand dribble. On command lift legs and bring ball under to left hand. Continue back and forth.

• *Merry-go-round:* Sit down with legs extended. Begin with right-hand dribble; bring ball around back to left hand; then under legs to right hand. Continue circle. Then reverse.

• *Back and forth:* Sit down; dribble right-handed and bring ball back and forth behind back.

• *Sleeper:* Lie down and dribble with right hand. On command sit up; bring ball under legs to left hand; lie down and continue dribble. Repeat.

• *Tom-Tom:* Sit down with legs extended and spread; place ball between legs; keep ball alive by dribbling quickly. Alternate hands; play a tune on ball; beat tom-tom.

• *Drop-ball:* Begin by bringing ball in left hand around left leg; slap ball between legs with both hands; drop ball and then catch it after bounce by reversing hands. Now bring ball around behind right leg with right hand to front. Now repeat.

Phase 3: Dribble with two basketballs.

• *Two basketballs:* Dribble them together about waist high in a nice and easy cadence. On command bring them lower; then as low as you can go; continue to dribble low and high, changing cadence.

● *Two basketballs:* Bounce them together about waist high; exchange balls by bringing one to the front and the other to rear. Continue and then reverse.

● *Piston drill:* Begin by placing one ball to floor; while it is coming up, other ball should be put to floor. Keep balls going by using a piston pumping motion.

● *Stop and go:* Bounce together. Begin with forward hand; stop and go on command.

● *Stop and go crossing over:* Same as above but stop and go crossing balls over.

● *Kneel dribble:* Kneel and do same drills as in stand-up position—together in cadence; piston drill; stop and go cross over.

● *Standing dribble:* Take standing position with stride stance. Dribble left-handed while other ball is being brought around right leg in circles with right hand. Reverse procedure.

● *Dribble both balls:* Dribble both balls at once and bring them around back and through legs at the same time.

● *Dribble both balls:* Dribble both balls at once and bring them from front to back through legs.

BALL-HANDLING CHALLENGES

● *Windmill (one ball):* Take shoulder-width stance. Object is to keep ball between feet on dribble. Begin by placing ball to floor with right hand.

> Note: The second dribble is with the left hand as right hand goes behind right leg for third dribble. The fourth dribble is with left hand behind left leg. Continue with a 1-2-3-4 cadence. Two dribbles in the front and two dribbles to the rear.

● *Toss and catch:* Toss ball over head with two hands. Step forward with right or left foot and catch ball behind back.

● *The "impossible" catch:* Toss ball over head so that it will fall close behind you. Just as the ball passes to the rear of the head stoop quickly forward and bring the hands and arms between the legs to catch the ball.

Tip: Timing is very important. If you stoop too soon the ball will hit your rump.

● *One hand "quickie":* Take stride stance and hold ball in right hand with arm held across the thigh. Toss ball into air and bring right hand under thigh to catch the ball.

Note: As soon as ball is caught flip it up and catch it again. Repeat as often as you desire, quickly. Switch to opposite leg.

● *Ricochet:* Stand with feet spread about shoulder-width apart. Hold ball chest high with arms extended. Bring ball down between legs; bring hands behind back and catch ball.

Tip: Keeping the arms extended and bringing the ball to the floor directly between the arms forms perfect angle so that no accident will occur.

CONCLUSION

These drills have worked for us over the years. At times we eliminate some and add others—or develop our own form of drill. The important thing is practice for better dribbling and ball handling.

9

Harley "Skeeter" Swift

Assistant Basketball Coach
Armstrong State College
Savannah, Georgia

Clay Estes

Head Basketball Coach
McLean High School
McLean, Virginia

BALL-HANDLING DRILLS
TO DEVELOP A PLAYER'S
FULL POTENTIAL

Harley Swift has had an illustrious professional career and is now assistant basketball coach at Armstrong State College. Clay Estes is the head basketball coach at McLean High School. His teams have won 175 games and three district titles in sixteen seasons. He has twice been honored as Coach-of-the-Year.

Here are drills that will help your players become efficient, confident ball handlers. Without the ability to handle the ball, your players cannot run the team offense, beat anyone one-on-one, drive for the full-speed lay-up, or free themselves for the quick jumper. These drills can help your players reach their full potential, but your players must work on them 15 to 30 minutes a day.

CORRECT RIGHT-HAND DRIBBLING

1. Legs underneath shoulders, slightly bent (Photo 1).
2. Weight on the balls of feet.
3. Head up, looking straight ahead—not at ball.
4. Keep left arm in front to protect the ball from the defensive man.
5. Dribble with fingertips only.
6. Keep body low.

Photo 1

CONCENTRATION DRIBBLE DRILL

1. Start in correct dribbling position (Photo 1), dribbling with the right hand and fingertips.
2. While dribbling, sit on the floor (Photos 2 and 3), keeping the ball moving using the fingertips only, then the index finger only, and so on (rotating to each finger on the right hand until all of them have been used).
3. Lie back on the floor (Photo 4). With eyes closed, go through the same finger-dribbling routine that was described in step 2.
4. Sit up with legs extended together on the floor.

Bring the ball directly in front of you, around your feet and legs, moving it from right hand to left hand without bending the legs (Photo 5).

5. When you get the ball with your left hand, repeat all the steps that have just been described, doing them in reverse so that you wind up dribbling the ball in the standing position with your left hand.

Photo 2

Photo 3

Photo 4

Photo 5

RHYTHM DRILL

1. This drill consists of three- and two-bounce exercises that are performed while standing in the correct dribbling position. The three-bounce exercise begins with one bounce in front with the right hand (Photo 6).
2. The next bounce is to the right side with the right hand (Photo 7).

Photo 6

Photo 7

Photo 8

Photo 9

3. The third bounce hits the floor behind you (Photo 8). Use a "fourth bounce" to move the ball between the legs to the left hand (Photo 9). Do this exercise with the left hand, moving the ball around the left side.
4. In the two-bounce exercise, the ball is bounced in front and to the right side with the right hand. A "third bounce" is used to get the ball through the legs to the left hand. The exercise is repeated to the left side with the left hand. To develop rhythm further, try doing it to music.

WALKING DRILL

1. Start this drill at one end of a basketball court or sidewalk (Photo 10). With the ball in the right hand, step with the right foot and bounce the ball through the legs to the left hand. (Remember to be in good dribbling position.)

Photo 10

2. Next, step with the left foot and bounce the ball between the legs with the left hand.
3. Continue on down the court or sidewalk, alternating legs and hands. After this drill has been mastered,

make it more difficult by skipping instead of walking.

COMBINATION DRILL

1. Bend slightly at the knees, and hold the ball with
    both hands between your legs. Start dribbling it with
    your left hand and then your right hand (Photo 11).
2. Next, alternate both hands behind your legs, bounc-
    ing the ball, and keeping it in the same position be-
    tween your legs.
3. Remember to keep the ball in the middle, between
    your legs. Use only the fingertips for control (Photo
    12).

Photo 11   Photo 12

CHOO-CHOO DRILL

1. While holding the ball at waist level, bounce it first
    with the right hand then the left. Move your body
    closer to the floor with each bounce.
2. Continue to alternate hands until the ball is barely
    off the floor, yet still in motion (Photo 13).
3. As each hand touches the ball, you should say,
    "Choo." This will help you develop rhythm. Re-
    member to use only the fingertips.

Photo 13

SCISSORS DRILL

1. Stand with your feet spread shoulder width apart.
2. Step forward with the right foot. Keep the left foot stationary. While in this position, bounce the ball through your legs from the right hand to the left hand (Photos 14-16).
3. Keep the ball moving back and forth between your legs in a scissors-like motion.

Photo 14   Photo 15   Photo 16

CIRCLE DRILL

1. Stand with the ball over your head in your right hand. Move the ball behind your head to your left hand, using the fingertips (Photo 17).
2. Keeping the ball in motion, bring the ball down to your waist (Photo 18).

Photo 17

Photo 18

Photo 19

Photo 20

3. Still in motion, the ball should be brought down to the legs (which you have closed). Move the ball behind your legs, from left to right (Photo 19).
4. Spread your legs, while keeping the ball in motion. Push the ball behind your right leg (Photo 20); then circle your left leg. Now work your way back up your body.
5. When working on this drill, try not to let the ball touch your body. Try not to make any noise. Start slowly and gradually to increase your speed as you become more proficient at keeping the ball in constant motion. (You may begin this exercise with the left hand, too.)

Head Basketball Coach
Fowler High School
Syracuse, New York

BALL-HANDLING DRILLS
TO DEVELOP QUICKNESS

Hank Fengler has been coaching high school and college basketball since 1966. He first coached in the Brentwood (New York) School District and later at Cicero (New York) High School. In 1973 he was assistant basketball coach at Drew (Madison, New Jersey) University and was responsible for scouting and recruiting. He later served at Hamilton (Clinton, New York) College as assistant coach, and is presently head basketball coach at Fowler High School. Coach Fengler is the author of a book, *Winning Basketball with the One-Guard Offense*, published by Parker Publishing Company, West Nyack, New York.

At Drew University we believe in good ball-handling. Thus, we work extremely hard on ball-handling drills, which, we feel, accomplish the following for the players:

- Develop ball awareness (location of the ball).
- Hand-eye coordination (proper execution with the ball).
- Anticipation (recovery of loose balls, being near the action).

- A feeling or touch for the ball (needed for offensive maneuvers).
- Develop confidence (with repetition of drills).
- Execution (fewer turnovers).
- Agility and quickness (needed for all phases of the game of basketball).
- Conditioning (added result of repetition and players working to their maximum).

PROCEDURES FOR CONDUCTING DRILLS

1. Most drills are executed in the basketball position. The player assumes a semi-crouch position, on the balls of his feet and with his hands slightly bent. His back is straight and his head is up.
2. Each player wears basketball glasses and has his own basketball.
3. His head is always up—not looking at the ball.
4. Maximum speed is required for all drills after the teaching stage. Each player is, therefore, always working to his fullest potential.
5. Each drill is performed for 30 seconds. Scores can be charted to check improvement.
6. Vary the drills, the routine, and the team leader daily.
7. Ball-handling routines are usually performed before the organized practice.

DRILL PROGRAM

- *Spinning the ball on the fingers:* The player starts the ball in a spinning motion on his index finger. He may start the ball spinning by using one or both hands.
- *Finger-tip passing:* The ball is passed between each hand using only the fingers of each hand to do the passing. Both the ball and the player's arms can be moved from eye level to over the head and then lowered to the area of the feet.

- *Circle the ball around the body* (Diagram 1): The ball is circled around the player's body starting near his waist and moved up and around his neck. Then the ball is moved down and around the body to the ankle area.

CIRCLE BALL AROUND BODY

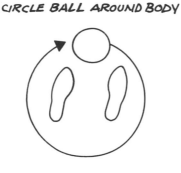

Diagram 1

- *Circle the ball around the right and left leg separately* (Diagram 2): The ball is circled around the player's right leg and then between his legs. After circling the right leg for 30 seconds, the same movement should be executed with the left leg.

CIRCLE BALL AROUND
RIGHT LEG

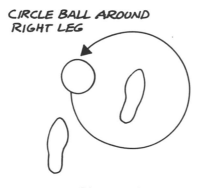

Diagram 2

- *Figure eight* (Diagram 3): The ball is moved by the right hand between the legs, and with the left hand it is

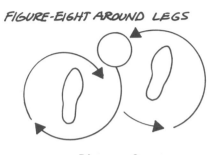

Diagram 3

brought around the left leg and in front of the left leg. The player's left hand continues the movement between his legs with the right hand being used to circle the ball around the right leg and back to the starting position. This completes one rotation.

• *Figure eight drop* (Diagram 4): The ball is moved around the outside of the left leg from the back to the front. Then it is passed in front of the player's body and around the outside of his right leg from the front to the back. Now the ball is between his legs at the back of the player's body. It is bounced once and on the bounce the player's right hand changes from the back position to the front position and his left hand moves from a front position to back position, grasping the ball before it bounces more than once. This completes one rotation.

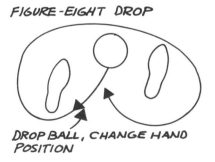

Diagram 4

● *Figure eight drop reverse* (Diagram 5): For the figure eight drop reverse drill follow the same procedure as for the figure eight drop drill except that when the ball is dropped or bounced the movement is reversed. After the bounce, the ball is circled around the outside of the player's right leg, around in front of his body, and around his left leg from the front to the back.

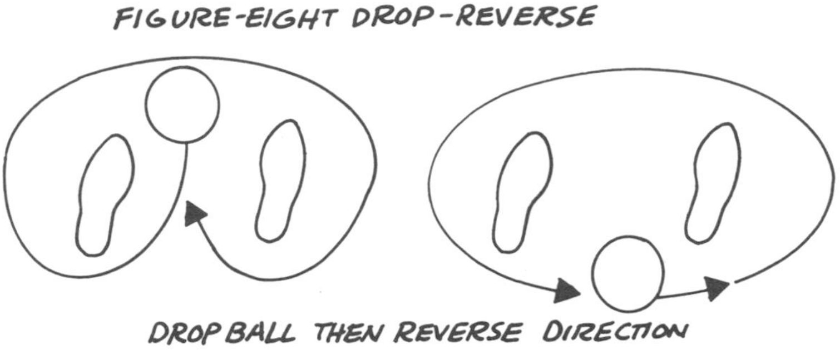

FIGURE-EIGHT DROP-REVERSE

DROP BALL THEN REVERSE DIRECTION

Diagram 5

● *Figure eight—running in place:* The ball moves in figure eight movement around the player's legs as in the figure eight drill. In addition to the figure eight movement, his feet are also moving up and down in a running-in-place motion.

● *Side catch:* The ball is kept between the player's legs, while his hands are shifted from a front to back position and from a back to front position.

● *Front-back catch:* The ball is passed from in front of the player's body to the back of his body between his legs. His hands are moved quickly to the back of his body to catch the ball before it hits the floor. The ball does not hit the floor. Once the ball is caught in back of the player's body, it is passed back between his legs and caught in front of his body. This completes one movement.

● *Front-back bounce catch:* The ball is bounced between the inside of the player's legs. It is bounced once and caught in back of his body with the hands. Then the ball is passed on the bounce from the back of the player's body to the front of his body and caught again. The movement is repeated.

• *Clap hands drill–ball behind the neck:* The player should release the ball, clap his hands together in front of his body, and then catch the ball in back of his body before it hits the floor.

• *Clap hands drill–ball in front of the body:* The player releases the ball, quickly claps his hands together behind his back, and then catches the ball in front of his body before it hits the floor.

• *Clap hands drill–ball between the legs:* The player releases the ball, claps his hands together once in front of his right leg and then catches the ball between his legs before it hits the floor.

• *Clap hands drill–ball behind the knees:* The player releases his hands from the ball, claps them together once in front of his knees, and catches the ball behind his legs before it hits the floor.

• *Pockets drill:* The player should throw the ball into the air, hit his front-pockets' area once with his hands, and then catch the ball in front of his body. He will throw the ball into the air again and hit his front-pockets' area twice. He continues throwing the ball into the air and trying to hit the pocket area as many times as he can and still catch the ball before it hits the floor.

• *Squeeze the ball drill:* The objective in this drill is for the player to palm the ball or squeeze it as hard as he can for a ten-second interval. Then he can switch hands and repeat the same procedure with the other hand.

• *Pound ball:* The ball is passed with a pounding motion from one hand to the other.

• *Crab walk:* The player walks, staying in a crab position, while passing the ball in and out between his legs in a figure eight motion.

• *Tapping the ball:* The player should tap the ball 25 times using his right hand and fingers to tap it and then do the same with his left hand. While the player is tapping the ball, he is also jumping in the air.

• *Side bounce pass between the legs:* To start the drill, the player will bounce pass the ball between his legs from the right side of his body to his left side. Once the pass has been completed, the player immediately shifts his left foot to the front position and his right foot to the back position. This shifting of the feet will occur after every bounce pass.

CONCLUSION

The preceding ball-handling drills can be most beneficial to the development of the players' individual basketball skills and quickness.

If your players possess fundamentally sound basketball skills, then they will be more apt to be prepared for the team's specific offensive and defensive patterns.

11   Joseph E. Flannery

Former Head Basketball Coach
Burlington Township High School
Burlington, New Jersey

AN ALL-PURPOSE OFFENSIVE DRILL: THE FALCON FROLIC

Joe Flannery began coaching at Burlington Township High School in 1964 when the school first opened its doors. After a few rebuilding years and a lot of hard work, the basketball program started to pay dividends—two South Jersey Group I championships and three trips to the State Tournament. Coach Flannery served as athletic director before retiring from coaching.

This drill—which we call the "Falcon Frolic"— incorporates faking, cutting, rebounding, passing and shooting, and can develop sharpness for the players who run it correctly.

Note: It is important to explain clearly to the squad the benefits to be derived from each part of the drill. Also, the coach should stress that each player must move in the drill as if it were a game condition. Here's how we run the "Falcon Frolic."

SEQUENCE A: RIGHT-HAND LAYUP SHOT

The squad divides into three groups and takes the floor positions as shown in Diagram 1.

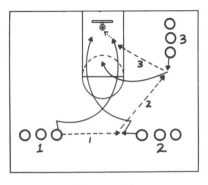

Diagram 1

Distances can be varied to compensate for teams with physical differences or coaching preference.

#1 passes across court to #2, fakes left, and cuts down the right side of the lane. He will be the initial shooter in the drill.

#2 passes to #3, fakes right and cuts behind #1 down the left side of the lane.

#3 passes to #1 and cuts just inside the foul line to take a position on the dotted part of the foul circle. #1 shoots right-hand layup shot. #2 takes ball out of the net, and the rotation is begun.

> **Note:** Players must step out to meet the pass. Drill can be run with the two-hand chest pass and/or the bounce pass. Pass to shooter should be such that no dribble is required prior to the shot.

● *Rotation:* Players rotate counter-clockwise as shown in Diagram 2. This part of the drill can be useful in the practice of recovery of the ball to get it inbounds quickly in the event the opponents use a full-court press following a field goal.

#2 takes the ball out of the net, steps out-of-bounds, moves quickly along the baseline, and passes to #3 who has moved out to receive the pass.

#3 passes out to #1 who is then in position to start the sequence again.

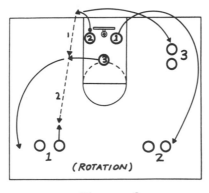

Diagram 2

Note: The overhead two-hand pass is used in the rotation segment.

SEQUENCE B: LEFT-HAND LAYUP SHOT

After running sequence A long enough to allow the squad to become familiar with the basic idea, the next sequence can be introduced as shown in Diagram 3.

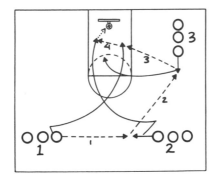

Diagram 3

The same procedure is used with sequence B as with A except that #2 becomes the shooter.

When #1 receives the pass from #3 he fakes the layup shot and uses an underhand shovel pass to #2.

The same rotation sequence can be used as shown in Diagram 2. #2, the shooter in B, can recover his own shot out of the net in this case.

> Note: All players should attempt to shoot with the left hand in this sequence. It may tax the patience of a coach, but a player who uses either hand well can be very beneficial. Once the players are familiar with the drill, each sequence can be run from five to seven minutes.

SEQUENCE C: SHORT JUMP SHOT

Sequence C adds one more pass to the drill as shown in Diagram 4—and #3 becomes the shooter.

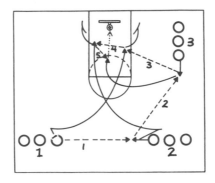

Diagram 4

With the extra pass in the lane, the ball-handling may not be quick enough to prevent a three-second violation. To prevent this, we have #1, after faking the layup and passing to #2, step outside the lane and assume the rebound position on the right side of the basket, and #2, after faking shot and passing to #3, assume the rebound position on the left side.

#3 shoots the jump shot from the broken line of the foul circle. The same rotation can be used as shown in Diagram 2.

> Note: The underhand shovel pass has been very effective underneath. The bounce pass can be used against opponents who keep their hands up. Form should be checked constantly on jump shots, fakes and rebound position.

SEQUENCE D: MOVING IN FROM REBOUND
POSITION FOR LAYUP SHOT

Following the running of sequence C, this final variation is added to the drill as shown in Diagram 5.

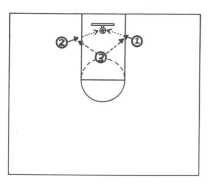

Diagram 5

#3 fakes the jump shot from the broken circle, and passes to either #1 or #2 who move in from their rebound positions to a shooting position underneath the basket on their respective sides.

This will develop their alertness in looking for a pass when they are in the area where the best percentage shot can be had. The same rotation can be used as shown in Diagram 2.

> Note: #3 must make a good fake on the jump shot in order to draw the defense to him. #1 and #2 must wait until #3 goes up for the shot before moving in to take the pass. #3 has the option of passing to whichever player is open. The one-hand overhead pass can be used off the fake shot.

The previous sequences were run from the right side of the court. This drill can be run with a left-side set-up as well, and it is advisable to change sides to prevent any possible stereotyping of an offensive pattern. The sequence A from the left-side set-up is shown in Diagram 6.

> Note: When rotating from the left-side set-up it is necessary

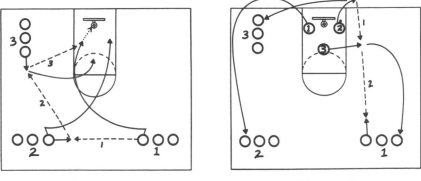

Diagram 6   Diagram 7

to move in a clockwise direction as shown in Diagram 7. It may take the players a few minutes to adjust to the change of direction the first few times the drill is used.

● *Optional rotation–using five players:* The rotation shown in Diagram 8 is for the right-side set-up. To get more ball-handling practice—and some player motion, as would be expected of a defensive player on a pressing type defense—as well as having #1 and #2 get used to cutting off a pivot man, this optional set-up can be used.

Diagram 8 shows the rotation after the layup.

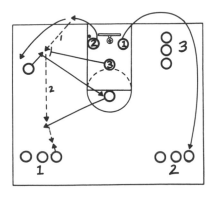

Diagram 8

#2 recovers the ball, steps out-of-bounds, and quickly passes to the corner man. #3 rushes at corner man in a defensive move. Corner man passes to pivot man cutting toward sideline. Pivot man hands ball to next player in #1 line who begins sequence again. #2 replaces corner man. Corner man becomes new pivot man.

Phil Faulkner

Head Basketball Coach
Katahdin High School
Stacyville, Maine

AN ALL-PURPOSE DRILL
FOR THE FAST BREAK

Phil Faulkner has been coaching high school basketball for the past eight years—the past four years as head coach at Katahdin High School. His teams have been to the Eastern Maine Tournament six years in a row, with one State Championship and one Eastern Maine runner-up.

The name of the game of basketball, here at our high school, is fast break or "run and gun" as it is known in today's basketball language. All our drills in practice sessions are aimed towards developing this theme—"the running game."

Note: We have not been blessed with a good, big man and with our tallest player going around 6'1" we feel that by running we can compensate for our size by getting the good shot (within 15 feet of the basket) and perhaps causing a few turnovers by the opponent who may not like to run.

PHILOSOPHY

With the running game, we can offset our lack of height. We stress the use of the fast break at all times by having our players get the good rebound position and the quick, good outlet pass.

My philosophy on the running game is good floor balance and a good outlet pass. You can beat a zone or a man-to-man by running if you can get to the offensive boards before the other teams have a chance to set up, and this is our objective throughout the season.

ALL-PURPOSE DRILL

The following drill is used in all our practice sessions. It is readily accepted by our players because it contains every aspect of the game of basketball—ball handling, rebounding, defense, outlet passing, shooting, boxing out, plus coverage by the defense in a fast-break situation.

> **Note:** Our fast-break drill uses all 12 players; they are divided into groups of 4 and execute the drill as a unit of 4. The objective is to match forwards and guards as a unit—and for each player to swap position after losing control of the ball or scoring. We try to line up a forward and a guard on defense at all times.

STARTING THE DRILL

We start the drill as shown in Diagram 1. Eight players line up under one basket on one end of the floor, and the other four players line up on the other end of the floor waiting to play defense.

COACH INITIATES DRILL

As shown in Diagram 2, the coach throws the ball off the backboard and the two players in the center rebound. The

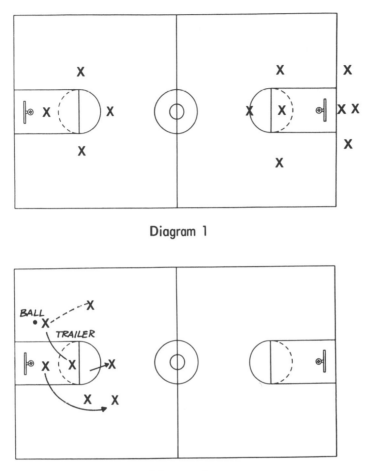

Diagram 1

Diagram 2

player who controls the rebound throws an outlet pass to the wing on his side of the floor.

WING'S ACTION

This wing in turn throws the ball to the other wing (Diagram 3) who has moved to the center of the floor, with the other rebounder (the one who did not control the rebound) filling this wing's spot—and who did not receive the ball on the outlet pass.

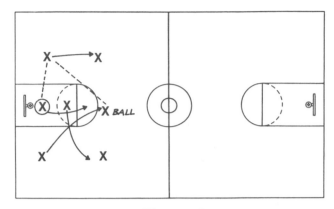

Diagram 3

SETTING UP FAST BREAK

As shown in Diagram 4, the player who rebounded must act as a trailer in response to a steal or a bad pass from his teammates. This sets up our fast break and everyone is running. This helps to develop the complete concept of a fast break with the ball in the center and two wings on the side and a trailer behind.

Note: Here the coach must stress good floor balance and ball control by the offense.

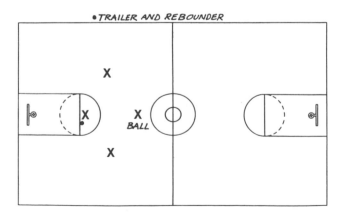

Diagram 4

GOOD DEFENSIVE POSITION

As the ball crosses mid-court (Diagram 5), the other players who are on defense must develop good defensive habits.

The point man stays with the ball until the first pass. His main objective is to stop the person with the ball and force him to make the first move.

As soon as there is a pass, then the second man on defense must follow the pass with the point man drifting back to fill his spot on defense. Again, good defensive position must be stressed at all times.

> Note: As soon as the ball is stolen, or the defense gets a rebound, or a shot is made, the team on defense moves on offense down the floor toward the other group that has set up a defense using the same procedure as shown in Diagram 1. The four who were on offense must move into a defensive position and the pattern continues.

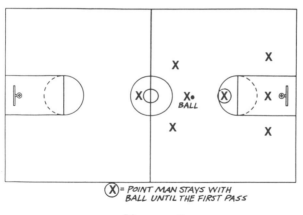

Ⓧ = POINT MAN STAYS WITH BALL UNTIL THE FIRST PASS

Diagram 5

DRILL EVALUATION

In evaluation of this drill—the players like it because of the game situations it involves, plus all the aspects of the game a coach could hope to involve in a drill.

For Example: Certain players hate to run wind sprints and we find that this drill takes care of the problem, without the players running in groups or one-on-one. Often, they do not think of this as wind sprints.

A coach may wish to change this drill to fit different situations, such as adding the wings to pick off any bad passes, or by changing the entire objective by eliminating the dribble completely.

PART II

DEFENSIVE DRILLS

1

Raymond Zsolcsak

Former Head Basketball Coach
Latrobe Junior High School
Latrobe, Pennsylvania

DRILLS TO DEVELOP SOUND DEFENSIVE FUNDAMENTALS

Raymond R. Zsolcsak's nine-year record as head basketball coach at Latrobe Junior High School is 76 wins against 26 losses, and includes a league championship in 1970 with a 13-1 mark. He left the coaching field for teaching in 1975.

Every coach says he stresses defense. But how many of us really do? Telling your players that good defense will win the close games and then spending only 15% of practice on it does not get your point across.

Note: The players will determine what is the most important part of the game by the amount of time you spend on each phase in practice. That is why we spend anywhere from 45% to 65% of our time on various defensive drills.

STRESSING DEFENSES

From our first pre-season meeting until the last game, we stress defense. This can be done in a variety of ways. Some coaches give awards. We do this also, but this alone will

101

not insure good defense. The player must be taught and drilled in sound, defensive fundamentals. The constant drilling is the only guarantee of a strong defensive club.

I will describe the drills that have contributed the most to the success we have enjoyed.

Note: We do not feel it is imperative for our players to use a prescribed stance or defensive position. We believe in giving the boy freedom to use his natural style—and as far as rules are concerned we have only one: be comfortable.

TRIANGLE DRILL

Divide the team into two groups and line up under the basket as shown in Diagram 1. On the whistle, the first two boys "shuffle" out to the corners of the floor (stress not crossing feet). As they hit the corner, they push off the outside foot and sprint toward the coach at the top of the key. Reaching the coach, they sprint backwards with their hands high. Reaching the starting point they begin over again.

Note: We run this drill every day of the season for approximately five minutes. It's an excellent conditioner as well as a good developer of defensive fundamentals.

GUTS DRILL

The team is divided into two groups under the basket, width of foul line apart (Diagram 2); coach takes a position directly under the basket and rolls a ball towards the foul line; as it reaches the dotted line, the two boys at the head of their respective lines charge after it (no holds barred).

When one has gained possession, he begins to dribble towards the other end of the floor, listening for instructions from the coach as to which basket he is to shoot his layup at. The other boy must attempt to get in front of the offensive player and stop him from scoring. Both boys return to the ends of the lines.

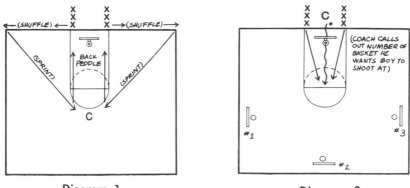

Diagram 1   Diagram 2

Note: The coach makes certain that the boys are evenly matched and must be in complete control of the drill because of the roughness involved. It is used primarily for aggressiveness and to help us decide whom to cut from the squad as it separates the men from the boys.

REBOUNDER SHOOT DRILL

The team is divided into four equal groups, two on each sideline at the foul lines extended (Diagram 3). The coach starts the action by tossing the ball up on the board and having one player rebound and throw an outlet pass to begin the 3-lane fast break.

The rebounder is the only boy allowed to shoot the layup. After the shot all three boys battle for the rebound. The boys are permitted to shove and push. Our purpose is to teach the boy to go after the ball; we are not concerned at this point with rebounding fundamentals.

The boy who gets the ball throws the outlet pass to begin the fast break to the other end of the floor. The action is continuous and a player may go as long as he can rebound.

Note: This drill, besides being a great conditioner, develops aggressiveness, getting the outlet pass out quickly, 3-lane fast breaking, and (very important for the younger boys)

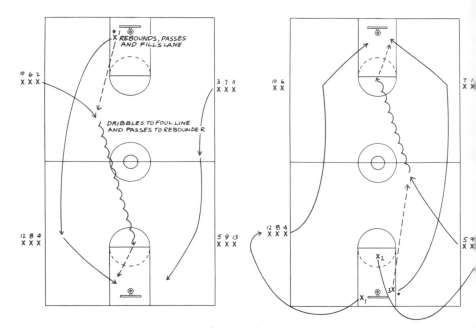

Diagram 3 (2 parts)

jumping straight up rather than out when shooting a layup. Again, the coach must be on the alert as the action can get pretty rough.

FIVE-ON-FOUR DRILL

Four boys are placed in a box formation on defense, while five boys are given the ball and instructed to attempt to score by driving (Diagram 4). The object is to jam the lane and force the ball-handler to pick up his dribble and toss the ball out; the receiver in turn attempts to dribble through and score.

Note: In order to prevent a score, the defense must react and move quickly to the ball. Every two or three minutes the boys are rotated so that every boy gets to play defense. This is a rather simple drill but we've found it very useful; it develops good team defense as it forces the boys to help one another and to jam the middle when playing a man away from the ball.

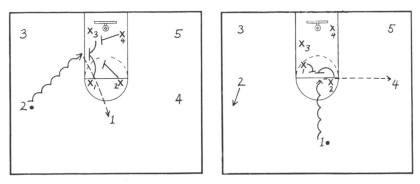

Diagram 4 (2 parts)

KICK OUT DRILL

This drill begins with three offensive players (point man, wing man and corner man) and three defensive players (Diagram 5). The point man, A, begins the drill by dribbling away from his teammates. As he is dribbling, X2 leaves his man and comes from behind to trap.

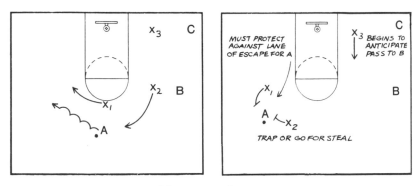

Diagram 5 (2 parts)

X1 must force the dribbler to turn right into X2. X2's job is to tie up the dribbler or to steal (kick the ball out). X1 and X2 must be careful not to give the dribbler enough room between them to escape.

If A, the dribbler, is able to detect the trap coming, his

natural movement will be to pick up his dribble and attempt
to pass to B, the wing man, who has been left unguarded. X3
must anticipate this pass from his corner. X3 must be careful
not to overreact and get faked out of position, leaving C
open.

> Note: This drill should be run as often as possible, as the
> defensive players need to develop their timing. We found this
> drill to be the most fruitful of all.

2

Ed Higginbotham

Head Basketball Coach
Harding Academy
Searcy, Arkansas

BASIC DRILLS FOR TOUGH DEFENSIVE PLAY

Ed Higginbotham attended Texarkana (Texas) College and graduated from Harding (Searcy, Arkansas) College. As head basketball coach at Harding Academy for the past eight years, he has never had a losing season.

When basketball season arrives at Harding Academy, our main concern is getting the squad ready to play as soon as possible.

Note: We are the only small school in our immediate vicinity that plays both football and basketball—and most of our boys participate in both sports. Thus, most of our opponents have played several games even before we begin practice.

If we are to compete successfully against such opponents, the best possible use must be made of our early season practice sessions.

Although as much time as possible is spent in shooting the ball, we know that we're not likely to shoot as well as our early season opponents. Therefore, considerable time is spent on fundamental defensive drills. Tough defense has won several early season games for us.

DEFENSIVE DRILLS

Among our defensive drills there is a series of basic ones that are performed every day in the early season. After a few days these four drills can be done in less than ten minutes.

• *Agility drill:* The first drill is actually a series of agility drills which is performed over a distance of about ten yards. A boy should be fresh and ready to go full speed in order to get the maximum benefit from it.

> Note: Included in this drill are the side-step, back-up, crossover and change of direction moves. The emphasis here is on quickness and proper defensive position. The boys should be low, with knees bent and back straight. The hands should be low with palms up. The head should be up.

The boys line up along the sideline in two groups (Diagram 1). Ideally, the seniors are in the first group. The first group begins on a set signal, performing the moves noted. When they reach the line (at mid-court) the signal is given to the second group—and they go through the same drill. Both groups are then in a position to do the drill going in the opposite direction.

> Tip: This is an excellent morale builder at the beginning of practice. A lot of chatter and hustle should accompany these drills.

• *Belt buckle drill:* For our belt buckle drill (Diagram 2), the boys form two groups—one at each end of the gym. There are two lines about seven yards apart across each end of our playing floor. One group of boys is between these lines on each end—with a defensive man facing each line.

In the rotation, the offensive man goes to defense and the defensive man goes to the end of the line. The offensive man runs the width of the gym floor, changing directions at least three times, and staying within this seven-yard area. He does not have a ball.

He should go all the way to the line at least once on each side. The defensive man must stay right in front of the offen-

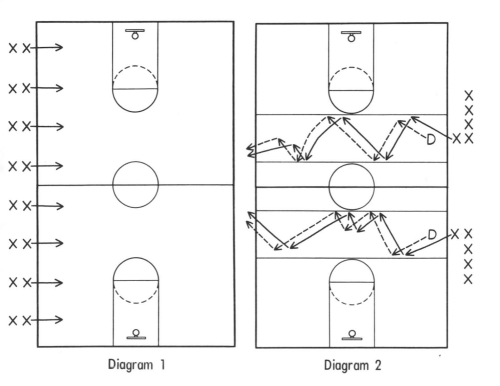

Diagram 1   Diagram 2

sive man—and see how many times he can punch him in the belt buckle (palms up) in his trip across the floor.

> Note: This is a full speed drill with emphasis on proper position, quickness, and an aggressive attitude.

● *Baseline closeout drill:* In our baseline close-out drill (Diagram 3), we place two lines of players on each end of the court. Rotation is from defense to offense to the end of the line. The offensive men (one on each side) are standing about 20 feet from the basket at the free-throw line extended. The defensive men are lined up on each side of the three-second lane at the intersection of the baseline and the three-second lane.

The first man in the line has the ball. He throws the ball to the offensive man and hurries to close out on him as quickly as possible—but under good control and in proper

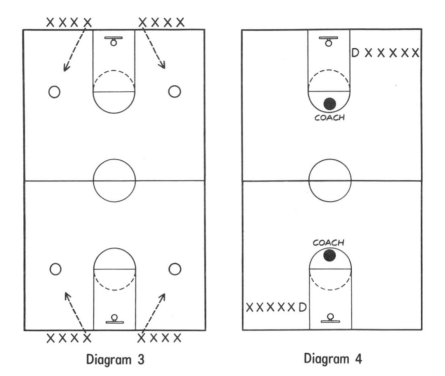

Diagram 3   Diagram 4

defensive position. The offensive man can shoot, drive the baseline, or drive the middle. We tell our boys always to favor the baseline—that is, to close out a half-man to the baseline side.

> Note: Each boy goes through the drill four times every day. The first time, the offensive man must always drive the baseline. We feel that this drill has been extremely valuable to us in keeping our players baseline conscious.

● *Prevent the pass drill:* The purpose of our last drill (Diagram 4) is to prevent opponents from receiving a pass in the scoring area. For our purposes, the scoring area is the three-second lane from the baseline to the free-throw line. Any time a good boy gets the basketball in this area—he will either score or draw a foul, so we feel that we must prevent this pass if our defense is to be sound.

Two groups are doing this drill at the same time, one on each end of the floor. Team members line up on one side of the lane about six feet from the base line. One man is on defense. Rotation is from offense to defense to the end of the line. A coach or student manager stands near the top of the key and attempts to pass the ball to the offensive man, who is trying to free himself in the scoring area.

Note: If he breaks across the lane, the defensive man should make him break low, behind him, or over the free-throw line. If the offensive man insists on going in front of the defensive man, he should drive him up to the free-throw line and then let him across.

Usually, the defenders will get beaten pretty badly the first few times they run this drill—but it doesn't take long for them to learn to prevent this pass in the scoring area. After running this drill in one direction, the boys set up on the other side of the lane and run it in the opposite direction.

SUMMARY

For the first few days, considerable time should be spent on these four drills in teaching proper technique and position. But after the drills are learned they can be performed in very little time. They should be performed in the same order every day.

We blow a whistle and quickly set up two lines for the agility drills. After these are finished, the boys are told to run their three basic defensive drills. They then split up into two groups, one on each end of the floor, and run through the belt buckle drill.

When this drill is completed, the one line of boys on each end of the court divides into two lines on each end and moves under the basket for the close out drill. Next the two lines on each end merge into one line on each end for the prevent the pass drill.

3

Billy Allgood

Head Basketball Coach
Louisiana College
Pineville, Louisiana

DEFENSIVE DRILLS TO PERFECT FUNDAMENTALS

Billy Allgood has been coaching high school and college basketball since 1953. His first assignment was at Meridian (Mississippi) High School. For the past seventeen years he has been head basketball coach at Louisiana College, and athletic director at the same institution for the past twelve years. His overall record is 221-205.

It is our belief that the training and mastering of individual basketball skills through drill work will, when woven into a team effort, produce victories. Because of this belief, we work long and hard on many fundamental drills.

Important Factor: A very important factor in teaching fundamentals through drills is to be absolutely sure that the players know what skills they are trying to perfect. Thus they can concentrate on developing these skills for the entirety of the workout. Many times, boys will practice with a "clock procedure" attitude. If the coach has scheduled five minutes for defensive stance, the boy is thinking of the time left in the drill.

113

It is the coach's responsibility to insure that the boy will concentrate for five minutes on learning the technique of a defensive stance, or whatever, instead of spending the last two or three minutes wondering how much time is left in the drill.

DEFENSIVE DRILLS

Naturally, all the drills we run in our basketball program are not original with us. We adapt drills to obtain the desired results. Because there are so many drills used today, we have limited our discussion here to defensive drills—and only examples of some of our favorites.

● *Stance:* In this drill, we place each boy in an athletic position that will permit him to move in any direction quickly, while maintaining complete control of the body. Each boy should have his feet as wide as or wider than his shoulders. He should have a staggered stance with the toe of his back foot about three inches behind the heel of his front foot. His hips and rear end should be down with his head and shoulders slightly forward. His arms should be up and ready to move.

> Coaching Points: (1) exaggerate a wide base; (2) turn heel of back foot slightly out; (3) do not allow a hump in the back; (4) mentally put the weight on the balls of the feet; (5) distribute weight equally on both feet.

● *Drill for assuming stance:* Our drill for assuming the proper stance is illustrated in Diagram 1. The first line will start jogging forward toward the coach and on a whistle they will quickly assume a good defensive stance. They will stay in this stance while the coach makes any correction necessary. On a signal from the coach, they will jog forward and again assume their stance on a whistle. After the first line has moved from one end of the floor to the opposite end, the next line will run the drill.

> Points of Emphasis: (1) boy should assume stance under control; (2) boy should maintain balance when assuming stance.

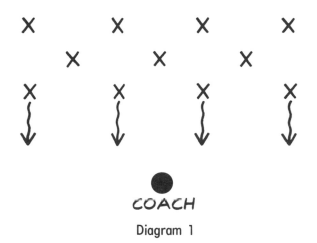

COACH

Diagram 1

● *Defensive footwork:* Anytime a player moves laterally, he should have a square stance (Diagram 2). Anytime he attacks (forward) or falls back, he should be in a staggered stance (Diagram 3). He will shuffle the front foot toward the direction he is going and drag the back foot. This holds true on lateral movement as well as forward or backward movement.

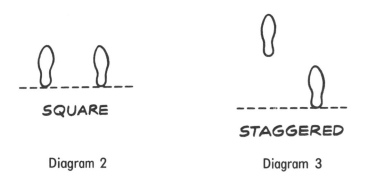

SQUARE

STAGGERED

Diagram 2   Diagram 3

● *Drill for defensive footwork:* In the drill (Diagram 4), the coach will point in the direction to be moved. He will be sure the boys are executing the drills and following the defensive footwork rules. When the coach sounds the whistle, each boy will set up a stationary defensive stance. The boy should not be off balance at any time.

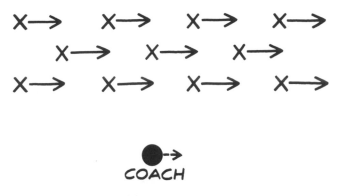

COACH

Diagram 4

• *Towel drill:* Our towel drill (Diagram 5) teaches a boy good defensive footwork and develops quick movement of the feet. The defensive man will assume a good defensive stance about four feet from the offensive man.

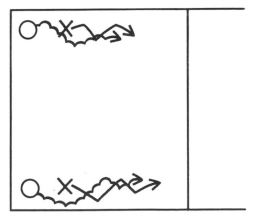

Diagram 5

He will grasp one end of a towel with his left hand and the other end with his right hand. The towel will rest across the small of his back or across his hips. The offensive man will start dribbling the ball down the floor, changing direction from left to right.

The defensive man must maintain a constant distance from the offensive man by moving his feet quickly. When the offensive man changes direction, the defensive man should switch his hips.

Coaching Points: (1) keep a wide base; (2) keep relative distance; (3) stay low; (4) switch hips; (5) move feet quickly.

• *Defensive punch drill:* The purpose of the defensive punch drill (Diagram 6) is to be sure that the defensive man does not let the offensive man freeze him. The defensive man should be continually working to control the man with the ball.

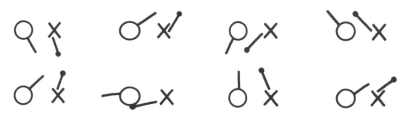

Diagram 6

The man with the ball will step toward the defensive man as if to drive to the basket. The defensive man must respect this fake and make the necessary adjustment using good defensive footwork principles. He must not commit his weight back or he will give up the jump shot.

The defensive man must attack the offensive man keeping his weight balanced so as not to give up the drive. During this drill, the defensive man is making constant use of his hands. This drill is similar to the techniques used by a boxer. After 30 seconds of this type of work, the boys should change positions.

Coaching Points: (1) keep a wide base; (2) never lunge; (3) keep hands busy; (4) never have weight committed forward or backward.

SUMMARY

The drills discussed here are but a few used in the basketball program at Louisiana College. We believe that the
learning process is greatly enhanced by repetition of skills
and techniques. This can best be accomplished in drills.

However, a boy can become an expert at running
drills—and still be a poor basketball player. Some talent must
be there along with a burning desire to improve and perfect
the game.

With the mastering of fundamentals through drills and
the desire to excel, a boy will certainly increase his chances of
becoming a better-than-average basketball player.

4

Bart Talamini

Head Basketball Coach
Cliffside Park High School
Cliffside Park, New Jersey

DRILLS TO TEACH DEFENSE

Bart Talamini has been coaching high school basketball for the past seven years—four years as assistant coach and the last three as head coach at Cliffside Park High School. His overall record is 113 wins against 58 losses, and includes one state championship; two sectional championships; two league championships; two holiday tournament championships. His teams have ranked in the county's top ten five years out of seven.

Basic to most successful basketball teams is a sound defense. The defense may be strictly man-to-man, strictly zone, or a combination of many defenses. The most important commodity here is that it must be played with not only the heart (or with hustle) but it must be played with the head.

> Note: What we mean by this is that you must have reason behind what you use in a ball game. You don't use something because it's popular or different. You use defense as an offensive weapon and also to stop the other team from defending you. In speaking to players, we like to call it "think" basketball.

ORGANIZATION

If your players know you are doing something strategically, they may better understand the game. They should then be able to react better to spontaneous situations. To do this, order and understanding must be initial objectives of your program from the beginning of practice—and commencing with your earliest formally coached teams.

• *Clinics:* This can be accomplished if you can get to students in the lower grades. Thus, we conduct periodic clinics for grade school students and coaches. During these clinics we stress our ideas on how the game should be played—and this carries over into the upper grades.

> Note: We stress playing the game and the importance of sound defensive skills. This attitude may turn into tradition and make winners out of losers. Remember, defense is difficult to sell.

• *Defensive essentials:* Use your defense or defenses with your freshman, sophomore and junior varsity teams until your players know all the variations as well as you do. The way to indoctrinate is by drilling all the essentials—such as stance, hands, feet, head, heart, etc.

> Note: The next step is to use your defense and be proud of it, and make it work for you. When your defense is working, so will your offense. There is very little a player can do after the ball has been taken away from him and you are heading for a basket.

• *Multiple defense:* We feel multiple defense is good, and we teach it. It gives us an edge on the opposition. To begin with, we discuss the values of defense and our defensive philosophy—and how it can be counted on at all times.

> Note: Whereas offense depends almost entirely on how well you are shooting—defense, we explain, can win for you on your poorest shooting night. Offense will not always be strong enough and can very often be manipulated by the opposition's defense.

Knowing various kinds of defense helps a player to prepare offensively for a game. If you play against pressure in practice, for instance, pressure in games will not be as difficult to accept or beat.

SERIES OF DRILLS

The following is a series of drills we use to develop good defensive players. We begin with a simple drill which stresses stance, foot movement and endurance. Before we go into any variety of defenses, it should be noted that we try to teach sound defensive skills. Before you can play any defense, you must be able to guard your own man, and help your teammate. You will see how the following drills accomplish these purposes.

● *Monkey drill:* The monkey drill is set up as shown in Diagram 1.

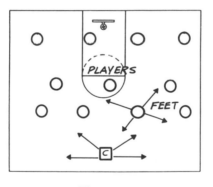

Diagram 1

1. Players line up in straight lines across the court facing the coach.

2. The coach explains how he would like his players' feet, hands, arms and eyes to operate. My particular opinion is that the players should assume the following position: legs spread to shoulder width; up on toes; legs bent at knees; tail dropped as if to sit down; hands directly outside knees; head to ball; eyes to coach's mid-section.

Note: Feet never leave the floor as player slides from side to side or top to corner on coach's signal.

3. The coach works on quickness and endurance, starting with three three-minute drills stressing perfection, from shorter quickness drills to longer (five straight eight-minute) drills.

4. The coach may use his hand or dribble to give direction. The dribble is good to use as an aggressive drill—roll ball and have players react to it.

• *Foot and head position drill:* This drill stresses foot and head position on full-court, man-to-man defense. It is also valuable in understanding position and rules of team defense.

Note: The court is divided into three areas: from side line to foul lane (A); from foul lane to foul lane (B); from foul lane to side line (C). See Diagram 2.

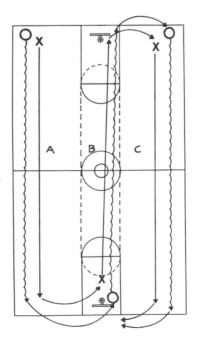

Diagram 2

The entire team starts in section A pairing up one-on-one. They work on a one-on-one drill with no hands (hands must be kept behind the defensive player's back).

The offensive player goes to extremes of each territory. As the players finish one area, offense and defense change. Each section is worked on for its own purpose—beating the man to right or left (sides A and C), forcing the man away from his strong hand (section B).

We are very interested in head position—it must be kept to the ball side. We feel this keeps us ahead of the offense and will eventually force a change of direction which could result in a mistake where we might capitalize.

> Note: Also stressed in this drill is that we must not touch the opponent for fear of a foul. We say that the opponent has a "communicable disease" which we do not want to contract. The drill is performed at least twice in each section for each player.

• *Quickness, desire and hustle drill:* This drill is a one-on-one drill stressing quickness, desire and hustle. Player starts one-on-one, full-court, no hands—trying to force a player away from a shot and to take the longest route. The offense is not to retreat.

If the defense loses the offense, he must turn opposite of where offense drove—run as fast as he can until he can set up defensively again. If the offense makes it to the foul lane area, the defensive player must throw his hands straight above his head; he can't foul or block the shot. We don't want contact. See Diagram 3.

> Note: This drill is expanded to two-on-two and up to five-on-five, with or without hands. It forces players to use such fundamental ideas as foot movement, eyes and head control, rotation away from the ball and a no-touch defense. We hope to force mistakes by a good "thinking" defense and not make mistakes by reaching for the ball.

• *Pitch and go drill:* This drill is used to develop a good two-on-three defense right from the opponent's pitch out (Diagram 4).

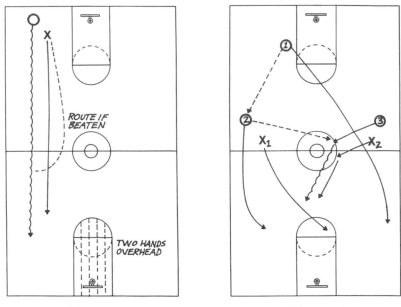

Diagram 3   Diagram 4

Players rotate clockwise, offense to defense. Offense man O1 pitches to O2. O1 fills opposite side. Defense man X2 follows offense man O3 across court. Defense man X1 picks up first pass as in a usual 2-3 defense and drops back to form tandem.

Note: We try to hold back the offense from a layup—at least until help comes.

● *Deny ball drill:* This drill is a one-on-one deny ball to the side. The players are placed as shown in Diagram 5. Of course, the drill can be performed on either side.

The coach has the ball and tries to pass it to the offensive player, and the defense tries to deny a pass as far out as possible. The offense tries to go back down and the defense opens up, facing the ball, drops the ball-side leg down and slides to the basket; as the offense returns to the ball, ball leg comes up.

Diagram 5

When play is complete, the offense goes to the defense and offense goes to end of line. This drill not only teaches players to deny the ball, but also to play the man with the ball and beat the man to the baseline, and stresses never to turn your back to the ball.

Note: In all the defenses suggested, it is imperative that the ball be kept in sight at all times. This deprives the opposition of the time needed to recover from a mistake. When the opposition makes a mistake, that's when we capitalize.

Deny-the-ball position means ball-side hand in passing lane, inside leg up and outside leg back—approximately dividing opponent's body in half. Eyes should be on opponent and ball at all times. As the player comes to the ball side to pass, you should refuse to allow any pass to go through. As he goes away, open up to the basket—that is, drop inside leg until you flatten out to avoid a good back-door pass.

• *Help and recover top drill:* This drill helps toward playing a team defense rather than merely a one-on-one. When your man does not have the ball he is less dangerous, so you must help. To do this we instituted a help and recover drill. The players are situated as shown in Diagram 6.

O1 is allowed to dribble to the center as if beating X1. X2 then jumps in to stop O1 until X1 gets back. O2 slides to the basket. X2 must get back allowing only a jump shot at worst.

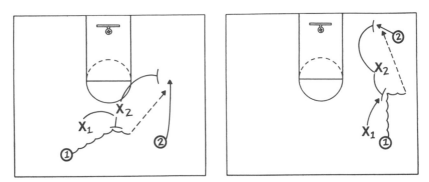

Diagram 6   Diagram 7

Note: Hands must be flying. The defensive player must get
into proper defensive position. Do not switch. This drill can be
used to the sides as well (Diagram 7).

The drill makes for good team defense and one where
players are not worrying about forcing men one way or the
other.

CONCLUSION

These are only a few of the drills that we use. They are
usually taken from game situations. If your boys can react in
a practice drill, they will also be able to react in a game situation. We feel that all games are a series of situations. The
more you can think of, the more you can prepare for.

As a coach you must break down every possibility and
work on it, whether it be defense or offense, structured or
free lance. The coach is a teacher and he must know what he
wants to teach, and teach it. If the players understand, they
will begin to think—and then you will have met your objective of having your team members use their "heads" as well as
their "hustle."

Note: Other drill situations used are—beating the post man to
the ball; jump switching; rotating to the free man; fighting
over the top. Think of more situations like this and create your

own drills for them. Get your rival's favorite play and defend
it as a drill. It will help. The important thing is to know what
you must defend, and how you want to defend it.

All of these drills have an important place in every
coach's overall plans—but without the will to make these defensive skills work your team may not be successful.

● *Motivation techniques:* Most essential in creating a good
defensive attitude is motivating your team to want to play
defense. As a coach, you are wise to discuss your philosophy
with your players and fellow coaches. It is good to note the
importance you feel great defense has for your team. You
should give examples of how it can work 100% of the time
—and how it cannot hurt you.

Another technique is the creation of goals. Some of the
goals we set are—no fouls for an entire game; shut a team
out for an entire quarter; realistically, try to hold teams to
less than ten points a quarter. All these goals are not reached
but do stimulate, and we feel this is a good method of instill-
ing defensive pride.

Note: You will then note how your players will begin to view
defense with more pride and begin to compliment one another
for a good defensive job. All this will lead to a new sense of
team pride and respect for your ideas.

We also feel that this approach to strong defense may
affect your opponent's attitude in preparing for you. If your
defense is devastating enough, the opposition may have to
practice so much offense that their defense may be lacking in
organization and readiness. This may be the weakness you
can capitalize on to help you win a game you would otherwise
lose.

5   **Jim Mogan**

Head Basketball Coach
Sacred Heart High School
Vineland, New Jersey

DRILLS FOR DEVELOPING AN AGGRESSIVE DEFENSIVE ATTITUDE

Jim Mogan is athletic director as well as head basketball coach at Sacred Heart High School. In his first year as head coach he led his team to a 15-8 record and to the state finals.

At Sacred Heart High School we believe in teaching one type of defense. We certainly respect those teams that have many defenses and use them to change the tempo of the game, but we do not feel competent to teach a number of defenses nor do we feel that various defenses are necessary for us and our style of play.

> Note: Instead, we strongly believe that players become skilled through the constant repetition of certain drills. We want our boys to work constantly on developing the same type of team defense—and the defense that we teach is the pressure man-to-man.

DEFENSIVE PHILOSOPHY

Today's players are intelligent enough to ask questions. Why are we playing this type of defense? Will it work? Thus, the coach must convince his players that his philosophy is the best one for the team. Once this is done, the teaching part of the coach's job becomes much easier.

At our first pre-season meeting, we tell our boys just how important a role defense plays in our basketball program. We stress the fact the the best defensive players will play. Boys who have only developed their offensive abilities soon realize they must now become defensive players as well.

> Note: This philosophy helps create a spot on the team for the boy who does not possess the great natural offensive moves but does possess the desire and determination to make the team a winner.

Our boys are told that in order to play our defense they do not have to be tall, strong, fast or quick. The most important quality we look for is aggressiveness. Every boy can be aggressive—it's pretty much a state of mind. A player must want to be aggressive—to dominate and control his opponent.

> Note: We strive to develop the aggressive defensive player—the player who has the ability to attack the offensive opponent and force him to make mistakes. From the first day of practice to the last, we spend 10 to 15 minutes every day toward this end, using the following basic drills for aggressiveness.

BASIC DRILLS

● *Combat drill:* We pair up our squad in six places on the court, as shown in Diagram 1. The boys select different partners each day. To begin, the boys assume their defensive stance with their hands on their knees, forehead to forehead.

> Execution: On the whistle the boys must try to slap each other on the inner thighs; they are not permitted to stop slapping or

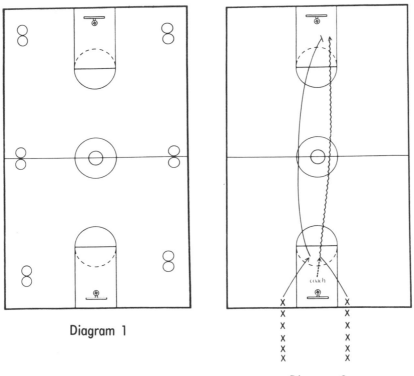

Diagram 1

Diagram 2

to back away. The drill only lasts 30 seconds but it develops toughness and aggressive attitude.

We are looking for the hard nose, aggressive defensive player, and this drill can help the coach spot such an individual.

• *Get it drill:* Players are situated the width of the foul line apart under one basket; the first two boys stand on the out-of-bounds line and the rest of the squad are out-of-bounds behind the first two boys (Diagram 2). The coach stands in the middle of the three-second area with three basketballs.

Execution: The first two boys step forward and the coach rolls one ball toward the foul line. When he yells "get it," both boys must dive on the floor after the ball. They are not

permitted to reach or bend down and get the ball; they must
dive on the floor to retrieve it. The boy who gets the ball
drives the length of the court and attempts to shoot a layup or
a close-in shot. The boy who does not come up with the ball
plays defense all the way down the court.

As soon as the first pair gets to the foul line on the
opposite end of the court, the next two boys step forward
and the coach is ready to roll a ball to them. After the boys
complete their trip they retrieve the ball and hustle back into
line to go again. Each group usually makes three or four
trips. We do not worry about contact, either in retrieving the
ball or in defensing the driver. We are stressing the fact that
all players must dive on the floor and come up with the loose
ball.

● *Three-man rebounding drill:* Three boys are placed inside the three-second area facing the basket (Diagram 3). For
this drill the players must wear weighted vests. Depending
upon the size of the boy, we will use either 10- or 20-pound
vests.

Execution: The coach stands at the foul line and throws the
ball against the backboard. All three boys must go for the
ball. The boy who gets the ball cannot dribble; he must go
right back up with it. He is not allowed to tip the ball; he must
come down with the ball and go back up with a strong move.
The two boys who do not get the ball become defensive
players, and they can, and usually do, use any means to
prevent the offensive man from shooting the ball.

This action continues until the shot is made or the ball
goes out of the three-second area. Again, we are not worrying about fouls; we are stressing aggressiveness on the back-
boards. Offensively, this drill develops the toughness to
make the three-point play. The drill lasts 60 seconds, but the
players receive a strenuous workout.

● *Go drill:* For the "go" drill the players line up at half-
court (Diagram 4), just as we would do a two-line lay-up drill.
The coach is at half-court in the middle of the floor with two
basketballs.

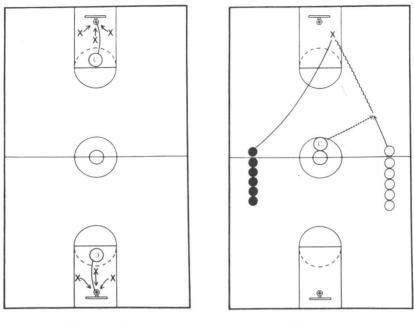

Diagram 3   Diagram 4

The coach yells "go" and throws the ball to the player breaking to the basket from the right line. The defensive player in the left line also breaks for the basket on the "go" signal. This defensive man must go for a spot marked on the floor, directly to the side of the basket on the right. The defensive man must establish his defensive position at this spot. We want this man to beat the offensive man to the spot, get set and draw the offensive foul from the drive.

The offensive player, after he receives the pass from the coach, drives directly for the same spot on the floor. The driver does not attempt to do anything fancy. If the defensive man has already established his position, the offensive man goes directly up and over him trying to put the ball in the basket.

Note: This drill serves two purposes: defensively, the players learn to get set for the offensive foul and not to be afraid to accept contact. Offensively, the players learn to go to the

basket and, even though hit, make the shot and get the
three-point play.

• *Reaction drill:* The players line up along the out-of-
bounds lines on both sides of the court (Diagram 5). Each
line is assigned a basket; the coach also assigns each player a
number.

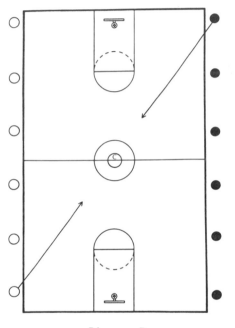

Diagram 5

Execution: The coach stands in the center circle and calls out
number 1—at which time both players assigned number 1
must run out to the circle and get the ball. The man with the
ball drives for his assigned basket; the man not getting it
becomes the defensive man, and he plays tough defense on
the driver.

The coach will continue to call different numbers until
each number has been called two or three times. This drill
lasts about two or three minutes and develops quick reaction
and aggressiveness in getting the loose ball.

CONCLUSION

Obviously, a team that develops a super aggressive attitude in practice must realize that mayhem is not allowed in the games. The coach must be very careful to explain the purpose of aggressive drills and to incorporate this aggressive attitude with solid defensive principles. Once this happens the coach has developed a winning defense.

6   Paul J. Frey

Head Basketball Coach
Elder High School
Cincinnati, Ohio

DRILLS TO MASTER DEFENSIVE GAME SITUATIONS

Paul J. Frey has been coaching high school basketball for twelve years. For the last seven years, he has been head basketball coach at Elder High School where his record is 132 wins against 27 losses. All told, his teams have won two league, two regional, four district, and two state championships. Coach Frey has received several Coach-of-the-Year awards.

As we see it, a player must be in excellent physical condition to play four tough quarters of defense. Thus, all of our drills are geared to conditioning as well as defensive game situations. When executing the drills, we also insist on 100 percent effort and pay particular attention to the proper defensive stance.

CONDITIONING DRILLS

All of these defensive conditioning drills can be used as part of your pre-practice routine, as practice fillers, or can be used to end your practice.

• *Alley ball* (Diagram 1): Divide the court as shown —free-throw line to sideline. The offense can't go out of the alleys. The defense turns the offense as many times as possible full-court.

Note: Three things can happen: (1) Defense must make the offense change the direction of its dribble. (2) Defense must take the charging direction foul. (3) Defense can force offense out of bounds. The drill is executed full-court because we use lots of traps all over the floor. We want the defense to take charge and create turnovers by constant harassment.

• *Cat & mouse* (Diagram 2): O is the mouse. X is the cat. The defense uses good stance, footwork and speed to stay even with the offense. The offense can go right or left and must use quickness.

Note: For this drill we go halfway around the floor and then walk to the end of the line and switch positions.

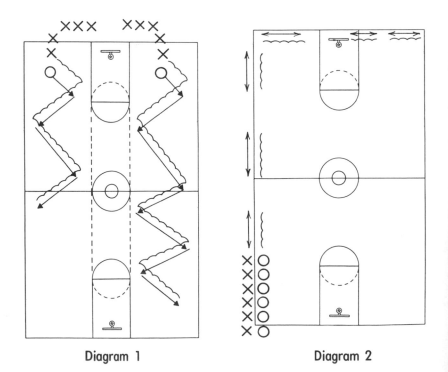

Diagram 1   Diagram 2

• *Whistle drill* (Diagram 3): The players are positioned on the half-court as shown. The coach stands in front of the players. The coach blows the whistle and points his hand —right, left, forward or backward. In a good defensive stance, the players move accordingly on the signal of the coach.

• *Open up drill* (Diagram 4): In this drill the entire team, using a good low defensive position, shuffle steps as quickly as possible—from sideline to free-throw line; pivot and go down baseline; across line; pivot; up to free-throw line, etc.

Note: This drill is excellent for stance, body control, pivoting quickness and especially for conditioning.

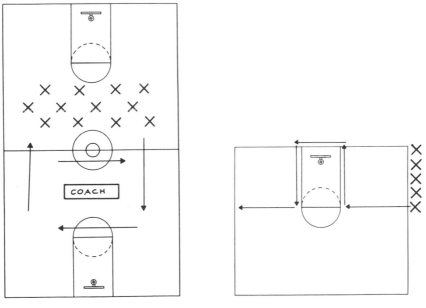

Diagram 3   Diagram 4

DAILY DEFENSIVE ROUTINE

We conduct a daily routine of half-court defensive drills or situations by which we "build" our defense. We start in

October with basic situations and continue this routine until our season ends in March.

Note: We build our defense using many combinations of 1-on-1, 2-on-2, 3-on-3, 4-on-4 and 5-on-5. In this daily routine we will add special situations that our scouting reports show we need work on. Figures 5 through 12 illustrate and explain these drills.

• *Denial of ball* (Diagrams 5,6,7): For the denial to forward drill (Diagram 5), the guard passes to the forward. D is to overplay O and not let him get the ball. If he does get the ball, he should only receive it high on the floor out of position. Do not let him get the back door cut on you.

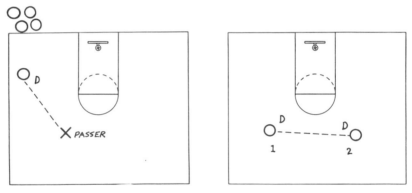

Diagram 5   Diagram 6

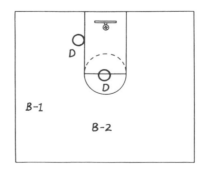

Diagram 7

For the denial to guard drill (Diagram 6), the guard passes to the guard. Defense 2 should overplay his man and not allow the direct pass. Make him go toward center court to receive the pass.

For the denial to center drill (Diagram 7), the pass is attempted from B1 or B2. D is to stay in front of the center and the only pass in should be a lob pass.

Note: On all lob passes we want the weakside man to come in and take the charge.

● *2-on-2* (Figures 8 and 9): For this 2-on-2 guard and forward drill (Diagram 8), we use the overplay. Denial players are allowed to switch, but they must "talk," play a series of 2-on-2 games.

Note: We stress all parts of defense, including both men blocking out.

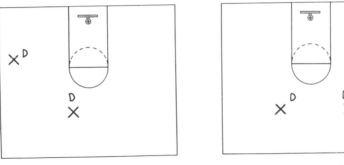

Diagram 8   Diagram 9

For another 2-on-2 situation using guards (Diagram 9), we stress pressure, denial, switching, talking and blocking out.

Note: These 2-on-2 can be with any combination of men— forward-center; guard-center. This depends on your needs.

● *3-on-3* (Diagram 10): This drill employs the guard, forward and center. X1 starts with a pass to either the center or forward and moves to the basket or to pick. Then you just play a 3-on-3 game, talking, helping, sagging, blocking out.

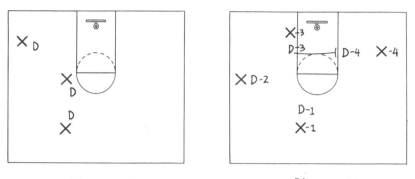

Diagram 10   Diagram 11

● *4-on-4* (Diagram 11): For this 4-on-4 drill, X1 starts with a pass to the forward. X2 stays center. X3 wheels to pick. X4 cuts to the basket. D4 is weakside and must do his job of denial. D1 sags.

Note: All 4 men block out on the boards.

● *5-on-5* (Diagram 12): This situation might be called "What do we need to work on?" So in your 5-on-5 half-court drill work against your opponent's strong or favorite offensive situations, always keeping in mind the basics of— aggressiveness; helping out; talking; denial of ball; weakside; sag; trap; turning your opponent; taking the charge; getting on the floor for the loose ball; blocking out on the boards —and wanting the ball more than your opponent does.

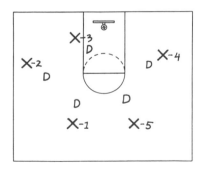

Diagram 12

Note: With the 5-on-5, run any offensive situation you want but be organized in what you want to accomplish. Use your game films as teaching aids and also video tapes of practices and scrimmages. This makes defense a challenge to your players.

ABOUT DRILLS

This past year, for the first time in my coaching career, we used a variety of zone defenses along with our usual aggressive man-to-man and full-court presses and traps.

And I found that any drill normally used for man-to-man defense was also extremely helpful when a zone defense is used. The important things are—keep all five players moving, always looking to double-team, sagging and helping, swarming when on defense—and giving 100 percent effort when on defense.

MOTIVATION

As we all know, a player must be motivated to play tough defense.

We sell defense by talking about it, pointing out in our films good and bad defensive play, and by devoting 65 to 70 percent of our practice to defense.

After each game, we honor the defensive players by having a poster painted with their names—and we make sure that our school paper gives coverage to good defensive play.

CONCLUSION

We stress to our players that anyone can score, but it takes a special breed of player to play good defense. We also stress that good defense will keep you in every ball game. In fact, good, sound defensive effort will be a big part of your offense during a game.

Note: Our state championship team (1972-73) averaged 10 turnovers per game as compared to 18 for our opponents.

This statistic is very important because we had at least eight more "offensive opportunities" to score.

Playing sound defense requires maximum effort for the entire game. So with this in mind, we condition our players so that they will be better in the fourth quarter than their opponent. One rule that is constantly emphasized is that no player is allowed to rest on defense; you can only rest on offense. We want all five players constantly on the attack.

In closing, our defensive philosophy is this: motivate the player, have him in good physical condition, explain to him what you are doing and why, promote aggressiveness and set a goal for points allowed. One more important point—you must be repetitious in your defensive drills in every practice.

7

Bill Leatherman

Head Basketball Coach
Staunton River High School
Moneta, Virginia

DRILLS FOR IMPROVING
INDIVIDUAL DEFENSIVE SKILLS

Bill Leatherman has been head basketball coach at Staunton River High School for the past nine seasons. During that time, his teams have been among the top defensive threats in their league.

A prerequisite for winning "team" man-to-man defensive play is the the squad, as individuals, to master defense. We constantly talk about and build our team defensive philosophy, such as ball-side play, weak-side play, sagging, help and recovery, etc., but any way we look at it, outstanding individual work within the unit is the key to our defense.

I feel a team using any variation of a man-to-man or zone defense can benefit from several drills we use daily during the season. The amount of time spent on these drills varies from day to day; it depends upon how well our players master the skills.

Approximately 70 percent of our practice each day is allotted to defensive work. There are many defensive drills that we can use to correct various weaknesses our staff detects, but there are four basic defensive drills that seem to reach most individual problems. We use two of the basic four drills each day.

SIMPLE DEFENSIVE STRATEGY

Our defensive style is not complicated, but there are certain rules we must master:

1. The *charge drill* teaches absolute protection of the baseline and the art of drawing the offensive foul, as well as the correct way of turning each play to the inside.

2. We never allow a cutter to cross the lane toward the ball, unless we have fronted him. We use the *talkside drill* to teach this technique.

3. The *trio drill* is used primarily by our guards to teach fighting over the top of the screen, sliding through and proper execution of the jump switch.

4. The *towel drill* is used to create mental defensive toughness and proper defensive play through positioning of the body. This is a favorite drill of our good defensive players—and they really can gain the respect of their teammates by demonstrating their skills. The best part of the *towel drill* is that it can be done by any player regardless of his ability—if he learns that "guts and pride" are the primary ingredients in becoming a defensive standout.

Our players really enjoy these drills. As they all are competitive drills, they are fun and challenging. I hope you will find them helpful when working with your squads. I know they'll improve your defensive game!

CHARGE DRILL

A chair is placed about two or three feet outside the free-throw lane and about six feet in from the baseline. The offensive player (O) begins about three steps in front of the defensive player (X). X passes to O and the ball is returned for a second pass. O will receive the second pass just prior to making his cut around the chair (Diagram 1). He is in-

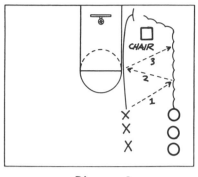

Diagram 1

structed to drive hard to the basket for the layup at all costs. X, after making the final pass, must hustle to the baseline with good defensive positioning. We encourage contact, but X is required to use the proper defensive position. X should not make the initial contact, but should "take" the contact from O.

Two balls should be used to keep the drill moving, and the players rotate lines. This drill encourages defensive toughness.

TALKSIDE DRILL

Players O1, O2 and O3 are in a triangle around the top of the circle facing the basket. O2 has a basketball locked between his knees. O1 (who has another ball) passes off the dribble to O2, who passes immediately to O3. O1 cuts across the lane to receive a pass from O3 (Diagram 2).

X1, the defender, must maintain a good defensive position on O1, by denying him the passing lane from O3. This phase of denying the passing lane enables us to condition ourselves to front all people inside the lane.

Note: In our team defensive scheme, if everyone fronts properly, we will always have a player behind any man in the lane, provided we have driven the ball to the side.

X1 is actually defending against two basketballs. This is

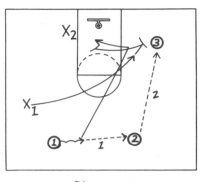

Diagram 2

designed to improve defensive quickness and inside recovery. O1 may make a quick return cut to receive a pass from O2, who uses the ball between his knees.

When X2 (under the basket) sees O1 cut back and O2 remove the ball from between his legs, he shouts "back" to X1. X1 must listen for this signal from X2. At the same time, he must maintain the proper defensive position on O1. In addition to serving as a defensive and a passing drill, the talkside drill also encourages our players to talk while working on defense.

TRIO DRILL

The Trio drill is appropriately named because our defensive players must use three different maneuvers to stop their men. The defense is always instructed to be close enough to touch their men (Diagram 3).

The offensive players, O1 and O2, are using the screen-and-roll effect. The defensive players, X1 and X2, must try to fight over the top of the screen and slide through with the help of their teammates. Or, if the front defensive man (in this case, X1) appears to be beaten, X2 (the back man) will initiate the jump switch. X2 will shout, "Switch."

Note: Emphasize to your players that X1 cannot call the switch. X1 and X2 must be working together and only the

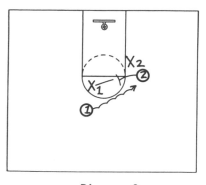

Diagram 3

back man can call for a switch. The switch is used only as a last resort.

Obviously, X1 will get more defensive work, so we rotate the four players into this position. This drill will help guards learn to stay a half-step ahead of their offensive men. You can use this drill as a two-on-two series for intersquad competition.

TOWEL DRILL

This is one of our more difficult drills for conditioning of the legs and at the same time for teaching positioning of the body while on defense. We use the entire court and have most of the squad active simultaneously (Diagram 4).

X assumes the defensive stance facing the offensive man who has a ball. X has a towel rolled up and placed around his neck. He grasps both ends of the towel and pulls himself "down" into the stance. His elbows are extended out to serve as antennas and for body balance.

O will dribble around the outside of the court in a zig-zag pattern going from side to side. He is instructed to stay within three feet of the line, while X, the defender, is instructed to keep his body in front of O at all times.

If X loses his balance, he must hustle back and assume his position guarding O. O will make a real effort to get

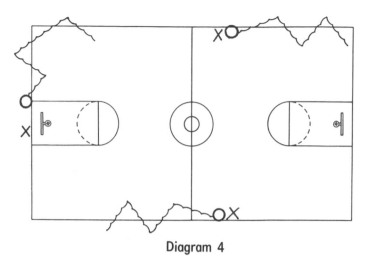

Diagram 4

around X. If X should lose his balance, O will not wait for
him.

Any player can perform this drill, regardless of ability.
Also, it can help many players gain confidence in their defensive skills. We have several combinations of players working at the same time and rotate the offensive and defensive
positions.

8

Mike Schrecongost

Head Basketball Coach
Medina High School
Medina, New York

TEACHING DEFENSIVE KNOW-HOW
WITH BREAKDOWN DRILLS

In eight years as head basketball coach at Medina High School, Coach Schrecongost's teams have won four league championships and one sectional championship, and have finished second in sectional play twice. They have made the play-offs every year. In league play, his teams have compiled a 71-28 record for a .720 percentage.

For any basketball team to be successful, the defensive part of the game must be sound. Each player must (1) want to play good defense, (2) have pride in playing defense, and (3) know how to play good defense.

WANT

The three points above are in their order of importance. To be good defensively, a player must *want* to play. If he is well coached and knows all the philosophy, but doesn't want to work hard, he will not be a strong defensive player.

In order for us, as coaches, to do our job properly, we must instill desire in each squad member to become a tough defensive player. In fact, reward the defense over the offense. Let the players see that the good defensive player has a spot on the squad and is going to play the game. Devote at least 50 percent of your practices to defense.

PRIDE

The second point listed above is pride. Webster defines pride as ". . . delight or elation arising from some act. . . ." Make the players see that defense pays off and that hard work will make each player a stronger defensive threat.

Try to give each player the opportunity to delight in the experience of overpowering someone through defense. Just keeping the ball away from a player by overplaying him properly can bring giant benefits in this area. As the player sees it is possible to do things through good defense, he will develop the desire.

As a player desires to play good defense more and more, and is rewarded for the effort extended, pride will develop. This pride should be encouraged and helped along. Do everything in your power to develop desire and pride in each player's approach to good defense.

Encourage each player, and therefore the entire team, to become defensive minded. Hope for the day when, after a game, your players look at the opponent's side of the score book *before* they look at their own. Build pride through praising a good defensive job done on an opponent, regardless of the outcome. Holding a team that is averaging 70 points a game to 50 points is a job well done—win or lose!

KNOW-HOW

The third point necessary to play strong defense is know-how. It is the coach's duty to teach each player sound fundamentals so that the player's "want" and "pride" are not built in vain. Of the three points listed, this is the coach's easiest job. However, know-how must be emphasized and explained so the necessity is seen by the players.

Note: Without know-how the player will get "burned" and lose some desire and pride. Proper know-how is a must for a player to continue growing defensively. He may get by on sheer guts for a while, but the better the competition the more know-how he will need.

BREAKDOWN DRILLS

I wish I had some secret recipe to relate to coaches on how to build desire and pride in each player, but I don't. I would, however, like to explain something I feel has helped my players over the past few years. I teach individual and team defense by the use of "breakdown" drills, and I very seldom scrimmage or put the entire defense against a full offense.

I feel that breakdown drills can be made tougher than the actual game situations that will be faced—theoretically making the team defense during a game easier than practice. This may sound like a strange approach but I think it has merit. Also, breakdown drills can be controlled more closely than scrimmages. Corrections can be made on the spot and the entire squad can benefit instead of only one or two players, because all players are working on the same area of skill.

To explain all the drills that we use would be impractical, but a sampling of them will, hopefully, indicate to the reader how they are used at Medina. The drills I will explain have to do with help-side defense.

HELP SIDE/BALL SIDE

This drill works on denying the penetration from a guard to a wing or corner, and it also develops the skill needed to play the help position when the ball changes sides of the floor (Diagram 1).

The ball starts at O1 or O2. If the ball is at O1, D1 must deny the pass to the offensive low post who may break to the corner or to a wing; but, in the beginning, he may not flash

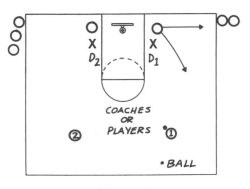

Diagram 1

straight up the lane. D2 must get two feet in the lane, and using the triangle theory of play off the ball, be in a help position to stop the lob pass to D1's man on a back door move. As the ball moves from O1 to O2, D2 must quickly move to deny the pass to his man while D1 moves to the help position. As skill is developed by the defense, free the inside offensive men more and more until crosses are being made, cuts are being made, and flashes are being attempted.

STOP FLASH/FRONT CUTTER

This drill isolates the weakside-flash post maneuver and backdoor cut from the flash (Diagram 2). The coach starts with the ball at a wing position, and the offensive players line up in the opposite corner. One defensive man is placed in a help position with both feet in the lane, using the triangle theory. At any time, the offensive player tries to flash towards the ball and receive the pass. The defensive player must see the flash coming and beat the offensive player to the spot he is trying to get to.

As the offensive player gets closer to the defensive player, the defensive player must close up his stance and deny the penetrating pass. If at any point during the flash, the offensive player cuts back door, the defender must open to the ball and front the player as if he were a cutter (Diagram 3).

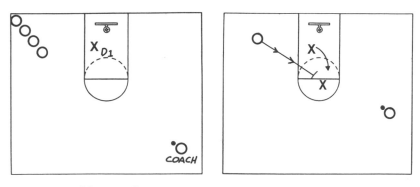

Diagram 2   Diagram 3

Note: When the flasher now cuts back door, the defensive player opens and fronts the flasher as a cutter to the basket (Diagram 4).

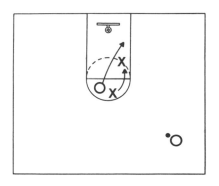

Diagram 4

DENY WING/STOP FLASH

This drill works on the coordination of the help-side forward and the ball-side guard or wing. It reinforces the stopping of the flash and introduces the help needed to stop the ball-side penetration (Diagram 5).

The drill starts with the coach having the ball at the point-guard spot with an offensive wing and defensive man. We also have an offensive man in the opposite corner with the defensive man in a help position.

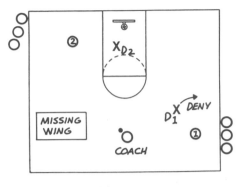

Diagram 5

D1 works hard at denying the ball to O1 without too much fear of the back door because he has a help-side man in a good position to stop that penetration. O2 can flash at any time, and as he does, D2 must let D1 know he now has problems of his own by yelling "Flash." When this occurs, D1 must still deny, but with more thought to the back door, which is an open move.

The coach should try to move the ball to either offensive man at any time, and if O2 does get the ball on a flash, O1 and O2 go 2-on-2 against D1 and D2. D1 must be able to stop the quick back-door pass from O2 to O1 off the flash move.

STOP FLASH/HELP BASE LINE/RECOVER TO POST

This drill puts the help responsibility fully on the shoulders of the help-side forward. He now must handle all situations explained up to this point and stop the penetration by the guard or corner man after beating his defender. This drill truly shows the great team possibilities of the help-side defense (Diagram 6).

The drill starts with the coach having the ball at a wing position, an offensive man in the corner with no defense, an offensive man in the opposite corner, and a defensive man in the help position playing the triangle theory on O1. O1 tries to flash, and D1 must stop the flash and front the cutter, as in the last two drills.

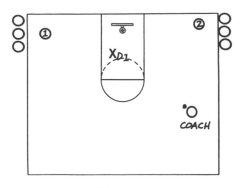

Diagram 6

If O1 does get a pass from the coach, he plays one-on-one against D1. If the pass to O1 cannot be made at any point during the drill, the coach can throw the ball to O2. It is assumed that O2 is either a guard who has beaten his defender toward the baseline or a corner man who has also beaten his man. In either case, he is open and moving toward the basket.

D1 should release his responsibility on O1 and get to the baseline to stop the penetration. D1 should get in a position so as to draw the charge, or attempt to block the shot. I feel that the charge is the best choice at this point and that D1 can get there if he practices it.

O2 cannot start driving the baseline until he has received the ball and cannot wheel and deal. He must move directly toward the basket until his penetration is stopped by D1.

Now, O2 has two choices, shoot the jump shot or pass back out to O1, who is loose and in the opening at the top of the key. If O2 shoots, D1 boxes out and goes for the rebound; O1 is not allowed in the play. If O2 passes to O1, D1 must recover to his own man and try to stop O1. At this point, O2 is not allowed in the play anymore—assuming his defender has recovered and he no longer is open on the baseline. O1 and D1 then play it out one-on-one.

In this drill, at first, it is difficult for D1 to get all his responsibilities coordinated, but with practice, he will soon have no trouble. The coach can limit some of the possibilities at first to make D1's job easier.

GUARD IN THE HOLE

This drill goes one step beyond the previous drill by bringing in to play the help-side guard and his responsibilities on an inside penetration. The drill is hard to explain but easy to see once it is put on the floor (Diagram 7).

The drill starts by adding a point guard and a defender to the previous drill personnel. We also put an offensive player, O4, out of bounds about five feet outside the foul lane, with no defender. O3 starts with the ball. He may pass to O1 on a flash or to the coach on the wing. O2 and O4 are not eligible pass receivers for O3. D2 must play strong defense on O3 at all times he has the ball. However when the coach or O1 has the ball, D2 must assume a help position in keeping with the theory of stopping penetration.

Since passes from the coach or O1 to O3 are not penetrating, we will allow them, and put D2 in a help position. These types of passes are made for the first part of the drill to get D2 reacting. D1 has the same responsibilities he had in previous drills, namely to stop the pass to the flash post.

Any time the coach has the ball (D2 is now in a help position with one foot in the lane, playing the triangle-off-the-ball theory), he may pass to O2. At this point, O3 is out of the play, and O4 steps onto the court. Also, no matter where O1 is, he immediately goes to the high post (Diagram 8).

O2 will drive the baseline, with the same responsibilities he had in the previous drill, and D1 will stop the penetration. D2 must now drop down the lane (in the hole) and stop any pass along the baseline from O2 to O4. At this point, D1 is stopping the loose man, and D2 is rotating in the hole to help on D1's man (Diagram 9).

O2 may shoot or pass. If O2 passes out to O1, D2 must now release from O4 and recover to his own man. O1 has actually replaced O3 for simplicity in the running of the drill. At this point, D1 also must recover to his own man, now O4. O2 is out of the play (assuming his man has recovered and he is no longer open or penetrating). O1 and O4 then play two-on-two against D1 and D2 (Diagram 10).

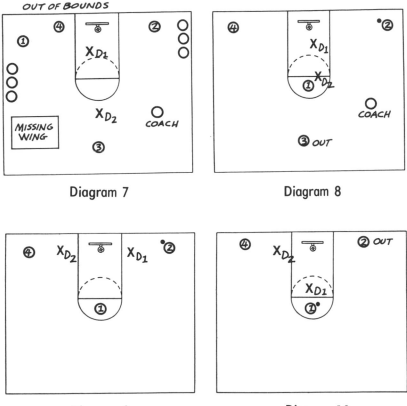

Diagram 7   Diagram 8

Diagram 9   Diagram 10

Note: I have found this drill a great help in coordinating the help outside with the help inside. As in the other drills, the coach can control the activity until D1 and D2 are more sure of their responsibilities.

In conclusion, I would like to say that all of our breakdown drills are *actual maneuvers* that happen in ball games. All we have done is isolate areas and work on them.

If you have an area of team defense you feel needs work, devise a breakdown drill that simulates that part of the game, and drill or build until it is no longer a weakness. I cannot take credit for all the drills we have and use, but I do think the idea of teaching know-how through breakdown drills has helped the defensive program at Medina.

In fact, we believe so strongly in this idea, that we use four defensive breakdown drills as part of our pre-game on-floor warm-up. The squad seems to feel that they are more ready to compete at the opening of the game and are better warmed-up than with just offensive-shooting and passing drills.

9   Johnny A. McCalpine

Head Basketball Coach
East Perry High School
Selma, Alabama

DEFENSIVE POSITION:
IDEAS AND DRILLS

As head basketball coach at East Perry High School, Johnny McCalpine has a five-year record of 111 wins against 47 losses. This includes a state championship (1974); state runner-up (1973); region championships (1973 and 1974); region runner-up (1972); area championships (1972, 1973, 1974). Personal honors include state Coach-of-the-Year (1974); state All-Star Coach (1973 and 1974); Conference Coach-of-the-Year (1973).

At East Perry High School, all defense must start with the very best position possible. It's our belief that to attempt defense without proper position is to start with a handicap that will prove most costly.

Note: We try never to give up layup shots and we strive to force all shots out at least 25 feet. To do this to perfection is almost impossible—still, the closer to perfection we get, the closer we will be to success.

We never want to be put in a position where we are forced to react to the offense; we would rather the offense be forced to react to our defense.

1-3-1 OR 2-1-2

We play either a 1-3-1 or a 2-1-2 for two reasons:

1. We always want to pressure the man with the ball. The offense decides whether we will be in a 1-3-1 or a 2-1-2 based on whether they are in a point offense or a two-guard offense. This makes it easier for our perimeter match-ups and makes it possible always to have man-on-man pressure on the man with the ball.

> Note: We feel that the three men closest to the ball must have man-to-man coverage; and we match-up accordingly, with the remaining two players making the necessary adjustments in relationship to the other offensive players and the position of the ball.

2. We always like to keep a man in the middle. His main responsibilities are to support the perimeter men on all attempts for a drive to the basket, keep the middle passing lanes cut off, and match-up on his man when the situation calls for it.

> Note: With a team that moves a lot our defense becomes more zone, but with a team that moves very little it becomes a very aggressive man-to-man with help.

DEFENSIVE TENDENCIES

We spend a great deal of time trying to develop the following four tendencies on defense:

1. Positioning
2. Aggressiveness
3. Help
4. Avoiding unnecessary fouls

It's our belief that all of this emphasis helps our offense in the following ways: first, it conditions the offense to play against good defense; second, it makes teching offensive fundamentals easy because they become necessary for survival in day-to-day combat with good defense.

DRILL PROGRAM

We try to develop the tendencies we desire through a special drill program. Here are a few of our favorite drills.

• *One-on-one half-court* (Diagram 1): We run this drill one-on-one from half-court. The players line up as shown with their hands behind their backs. The drill emphasizes that defense is played with the feet, and that without a proper stance good defense is impossible.

Note: Things we try to correct with this drill are: crossing of the feet, weight distribution, maintaining good position, and avoiding the habit of reaching when trying to cut off a drive toward the basket.

While all of these weaknesses show up in the drill, the most glaring is the tendency to grab a driver rather than cut him off by quick feet movement. A major point of emphasis here is always to make the offensive player aware of the charge.

• *One-on-one full-court* (Diagram 2): Here, we start from one end of the court and try to match our best defensive players against our best offensive players. We want our defensive player to play to the ball side, attempting to force the dribbler into as many reverse pivots as possible—thereby forcing him to use both hands.

• *Three-on-three half-court* (Diagrams 3 and 4): In this drill, as in our defense, we never want the ball dribbled into the free-throw circle or lane. Therefore, we instruct X1 to play his man very aggressively and force him either left to right, but never allow him to penetrate down the middle, and to pressure all passes away from the middle. When the ball is passed, we make the above adjustments.

Note: It is the responsibility of the remaining two players to adjust themselves properly in relation to the position of the ball and the other two players. The only problem here is to point out to them what you consider proper position.

Against a 2-1-2 or 1-3-1 offense, we would automatically be matched up man-for-man, but odd alignments like the

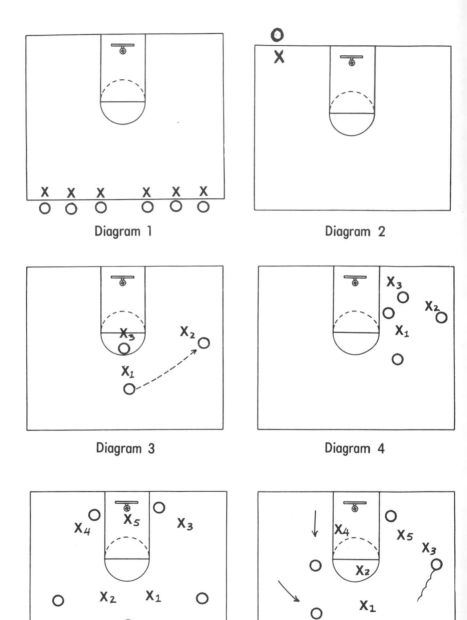

Diagram 1

Diagram 2

Diagram 3

Diagram 4

Diagram 5

Diagram 6

one above called for adjustments, which we made in the above manner. We feel that much time should be spent teaching your players to make the proper adjustments to odd formations.

> Note: The man with the ball and the two offensive men closest to the ball are played man-for-man, and the remaining two players have made the proper adjustments.

● *Five-on-five half-court* (Diagrams 5 and 6): When running this drill, we use a rebound ring and practice rebounding under game-like conditions. We feel that this is especially important because we get practice rebounding from the position we will be in as a result of making our adjustments, and because defense ends only after the ball is in our possession.

George Noch

Head Basketball Coach
Mt. Pleasant High School
Mt. Pleasant, Michigan

DEFENSIVE DRILLS FOR
A FEEDER SYSTEM

George Noch, the winningest coach in Mt. Pleasant (Michigan) High School's history, has a career coaching record of 205 wins and 103 losses. His teams have won six conference championships, five district championships, one regional championship—and in 1975, his team was in the state finals.

Here are drills for teaching good man-to-man defense. Each drill teaches and progressively develops your players' skills. Other drills may be used by the coach, but these drills are recommended as the foundation.

In addition to the drills' techniques, each coach should be aware of the terminology used in these drills. This is important because it allows coaches at all levels to use the same terms and describe the same actions. This makes for consistency from year to year, which benefits both players and coaches.

The most important thing to remember is that the techniques of defense should be stressed at all times—not just those times that the players are practicing them. These techniques should become part of the players' skills and part of the team's play.

TOSS IT OUT AND PLAY DIRECTIONAL DEFENSE

• *Objective:* To teach each player to use the proper foot-work when approaching a ball handler. The second phase is to teach a player to direct the offensive player's moves. (See Diagram 1.)

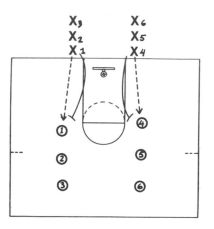

Diagram 1

• *Techniques:* One foot should be closer to the player being guarded than the other foot, the knees should be bent, the arms should be in palms-up position.

• *Procedure:*

1. Players X1, X2, X3 are under the basket on defense. Players O1, O2, O3 are within shooting range on offense.

2. Player X1 has the ball and gives it to O1. X1 must get to O1 to prevent the quick shot and any subsequent offensive move. Make sure that the defense approaches using the one-foot-forward shuffle.

3. X1 and O1 play until O1 scores or X1 gets the ball. Each player then goes to the line opposite the one from which he started (i.e., offensive man goes to the end of the defensive line, and *vice versa*).

4. After the correct footwork is drilled, the coach should have the defensive man dictate the direction of the offensive man. This is called "directional defense." The defensive man should:

   a. Make the offensive player go left.

   b. Make the offensive player go right.

   c. Make the offensive player go to his weak hand.

   d. Make the offensive player shoot outside, etc.

TRIANGLE OF DEFENSE

Diagram 2 illustrates the fundamental formation that the defensive man wants to be in, in regard to his man and the ball, after each position change his man makes. Several rules can help a player achieve his goal:

1. A player should always be *one step* off the base of the triangle or one step off the passing lane.

2. The formation should be *ball-me-man*. In other words, never let the man get between you and the ball.

3. Open up to the ball. You should be able to see the ball and the man you are guarding.

4. The farther your man is from the ball, the farther you may be away from him. However, always maintain your position one step off the base of the triangle.

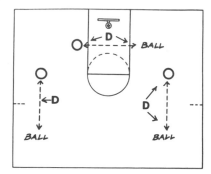

Diagram 2

ONE-ON-ONE WITH THE COACH

● *Objective:* To teach each player the correct defensive position in an ever-changing situation. (See Diagram 3.)

● *Technique:* The coach should not throw the ball to the offensive player the first time he gets open. It is better to give both the offensive and defensive men time to work before going in to the one-on-one play with the ball.

● *Procedure:*

1. Player O1 has the ball and tosses it to the coach. X1 is guarding O1.
2. O1 makes any cut he wants in any direction he wants. X1 must maintain proper position and prevent the pass.
3. On the pass from the coach to O1, O1 and X1 play until O1 scores or X1 gets the ball.
4. A player goes from offense to defense and then to the end of the line. The starting position for the offensive player may be changed to suit the coach.

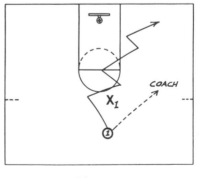

Diagram 3

TWO-ON-TWO WITH THE COACH

● *Objective:* This is similar to the previous drill, but more emphasis is put on beating screens and working on weak side position. (See Diagram 4.)

- *Technique:* A player should always strive for position on the ball side of the screener.
- *Procedure:*

1. O1 and O2 are on offense; X1 and X2 are on defense. X2 must not let O1 pass the ball to O2.
2. After O1 passes to the coach, O1 and O2 may make any cut to get open. The coach passes the ball to the open man, but only after several cuts have been made.
3. It is very important that a defensive player does not follow his man's fakes away from the ball. Switching should not be allowed at first, but should be taught as progress is made.
4. Additional screeners may be placed as shown in Diagrams 5 through 7. Managers usually make good screeners.

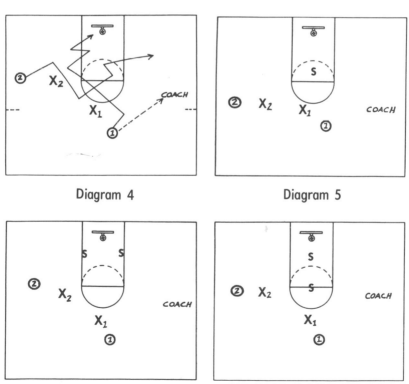

Diagram 4   Diagram 5

Diagram 6   Diagram 7

HELPING DRILL

● *Objective:* To teach each player to assist a teammate on defense and still be responsible for his own man. (See Diagram 8.)

● *Technique:* Make sure the helping player uses a shuffle step and maintains good body position. Reaching with a hand is not good enough.

● *Procedure:*

1. X1 must make O1 drive to the middle.
2. O2 must be in shooting range, and in the beginning, he must remain stationary.
3. As O1 drives, X2 must shuffle to stop his drive. When O1 passes to O2, X2 must return and prevent the shot by O2.
4. This drill then becomes a two-on-two drill, until the offense scores or the defense gets the ball.
5. Initially, O2 is allowed to drive to the basket. Later, O2 should be allowed to back-door X2 without the ball.
6. Diagram 9 shows the same drills in a guard-forward situation.
7. Diagram 10 shows the guard-forward-post man-helping situation.

CUT THE LEAD—FRONTING

● *Objective:* To reinforce the triangle of defense. To learn to prevent a pass. To learn to cover the backdoor cut. (See Diagram 11.)

● *Technique:* The defensive player must over-play on the ball side at least half a step. He must learn to shuffle without unnecessary head movement to see the ball. He must open to the ball or close to the man when the backdoor cut is made.

● *Procedure:*

1. Two groups go at the same time, but the offensive player must work to get open somewhere in the area

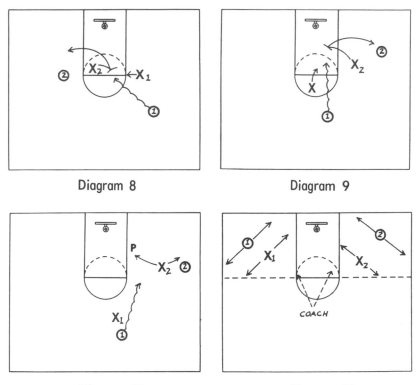

Diagram 8   Diagram 9

Diagram 10   Diagram 11

of the free-throw line extended and the free-throw lane line.

2. The coach has the ball and should not pass too soon. Make both the offense and defense work on technique.

3. On the pass, it is two-on-two completion. It will help if either defensive man yells, "Ball," when he sees the pass made.

4. Make sure the defensive man away from the pass releases and uses proper triangle-defense techniques.

5. You can add one or even two screeners in the key.

6. Players go from offense to defense and also change sides on the floor.

There are other drills that are very suitable for teaching and working on defense. Constant work in the one-on-one, two-on-two, three-on-three situation, both half-court and full-court, is very good. The key to success, however, is having the proper techniques taught early, reinforcing them at all levels, and never allowing them to be done incorrectly. Defense can be the foundation of a team's success.

PART III

CONDITIONING DRILLS

1

Ray Landers

A PHYSICAL DEVELOPMENT
PROGRAM FOR
BASKETBALL SUCCESS

Ray Landers has been coaching high school basketball since 1964 and has an overall record of 320-67. As head coach at Deer Park High School, he has a five year record of 152-33, including three district and two bi-district championships. He has coached All-District, All-State, and All-American players, and his teams have never finished lower than second place in district play. His honors include a Coach-of-the-Year award (1974-75) and All-Star Coach (1976).

The Deer Park Physical Development Program for basketball players began in 1970. It has as its objectives:

1. Improving jumping ability.
2. Increasing strength without interfering with agility and flexibility.
3. Building confidence through improved fundamental skills.
4. Increasing competitiveness of all players.

Our program consists of three groups of stations: The first group includes eight stations, and the second and third groups consist of four stations each (Diagrams 1 and 2).

GROUP I

The eight Group I stations center around the Universal Gym in our weight-training room (Diagram 1; Photos 1, 2, and 3). Players start with ten fingertip push-ups before beginning at Station 1, which consists of ten dips. Players then proceed clockwise to the leg press, lat pulls, leg lift, quadricep and hamstring lift, military press, pull-ups, and sit-ups.

After a player completes a station, he moves to the next one and waits his turn if the station is occupied. If it's empty, he does his ten repetitions and then proceeds to the next station. When the sit-up station is completed, a player waits until a group of four can be formed. This group then proceeds with the Group II stations in the gym.

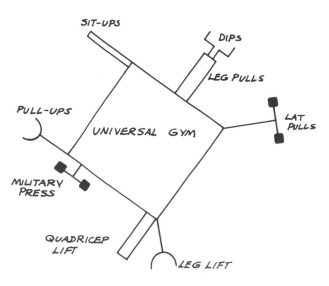

Diagram 1

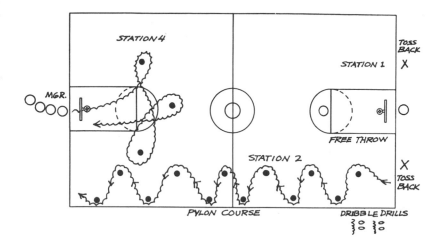

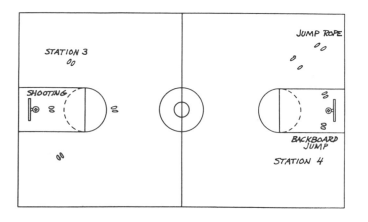

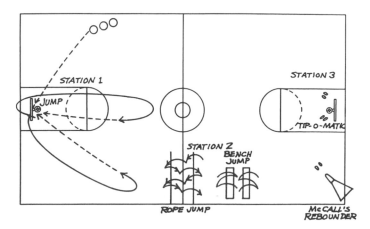

Diagram 2

Photo 1

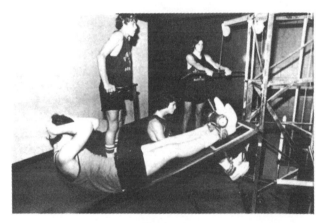

Photo 2

Photo 3

GROUP II

When a group of four players comes into the gym, an assistant coach positions the group at Station 1 of Group II. During each of the Group II and III stations, all players wear ankle weights to help develop quickness and explosiveness.

Station 1. Each group of four is split into two pairs. Each pair spends two minutes shooting free throws for form and two minutes practicing as many two-hand chest passes with the Toss Backs as possible (Diagram 3). The passes are practiced while standing at stationary positions and while sliding from left to right and right to left (Photo 4).

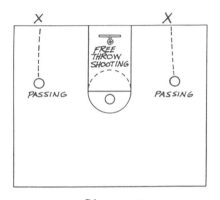

Diagram 3

Photo 4

Station 2. Again, players perform in pairs. One pair, with blinders on, drives down the pylon course as quickly as possible. The other pair works on stationary dribble drills (Diagram 4, Photo 5). The stationary dribble drills include:

1. Dribbling across the body from outside the left leg to outside the right leg with low, quick dribbles. Each hand is used.

2. Cross-over dribbling from left to right and right to left.

3. Dribbling a figure eight around and through the legs.

4. Dribbling a circle around both legs with the feet placed together.

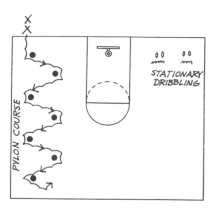

Diagram 4

Photo 5

Station 3. Each player must use the four minutes at this station to work on a particular shot each day. For example, the post men can work on a hook shot, fall-away jump shot, or power shot into the lane. Forwards can work on set shots or driving jump shots in their shooting area. Guards will use their time on jump shots from their area (Diagram 5, Photo 6).

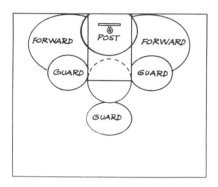

Diagram 5

Photo 6

Station 4. With a manager timing and recording the best time each day, the players must dribble a pylon course. This course requires agility and ball-handling ability to be run fast. The course is dribbled at least twice by each player. It may be run more if time allows. The course is run to the right one day and to the left the next. (See Diagram 6 and Photo 7.)

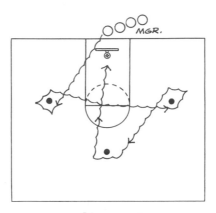

Diagram 6

Photo 7

GROUP III

Each station in Group III has as its objective improved jumping ability and better rebounding strength and timing. The players continue to work in groups for four minutes at each station. When a station consists of two activities, the time is equally divided between the two.

Station 1. The players begin in one line and execute:

1. A running jump off the left foot from the right side of the basket.

2. A running jump off the right foot from the left side of the board.

3. A running jump off both feet down the middle of the lane.

Players try to touch the highest spot on the board.

Note: Players must use the hand opposite the foot from which they jumped to touch the board. Therefore, if a player jumps off his right foot, he touches the board with his left hand.

As one player jumps, another begins running to the basket. This exercise continues until each player has jumped once from each position. (See Diagram 7 and Photo 8.)

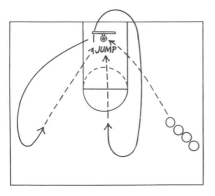

Diagram 7

Photo 8

Station 2. The group splits into two pairs for this station. One pair of players jumps off two feet over two ropes that are connected to the floor and rise to a connection on the wall four feet from the floor. Players begin at the lowest point. They jump continuously up the ropes until they reach their maximum vertical jumping height. When they can jump no higher, they jump backward over the ropes to the starting point (Diagram 8).

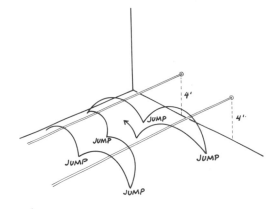

Diagram 8

Two benches are necessary for the second half of Station 2. One player jumps over a bench 25 times, jumping off both feet. The other player begins by standing with one foot on the floor and one foot on the bench. He pushes off with the foot that is on the floor, jumping over the bench. When he lands, the foot that was on the floor should now be on the bench and the other foot should be on the floor. He immediately pushes off with the foot that has landed on the floor, continuing this exercise until his partner has completed 25 bench jumps. When the 25 jumps are completed, the players switch exercises (Diagram 9, Photo 9).

Station 3. While performing at this station, each player wears a 25-pound weight jacket in addition to ankle weights. Two players work at the Tip-O-Matic placed in the basket. They must keep their arms up, tip the ball with one or two hands, and never allow the ball to hit the floor. They should always be in rebound position.

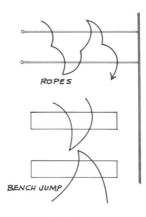

Diagram 9

Photo 9

The other two players take a basketball. Using the arm on the McCall's Rebounder for resistance, they jump, place the ball over the arm, and pull it down to the chest to complete a rebound. Without resting or taking a step, a player repeats these actions 10 times. The other player begins the exercise when his partner is through. (See Diagram 10 and Photo 10.)

Station 4. To complete the program, two players make 25 consecutive jumps as quickly as possible off both feet, with both hands reaching high to hit a spot on the board. At the end of 25 jumps, they rest and begin again if time permits.

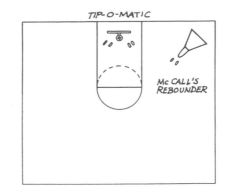

Diagram 10

Photo 10

Photo 11

The other two players jump rope for two minutes. When they have finished jumping rope, they change places in the station with the other two players (Photo 11).

This physical development program begins one week after the end of the varsity season (approximately March 1). It continues through the first week of May. The players work in the program three times a week. The other two days are devoted to free play, during which time the boys choose teams and play full-court games. With three playing courts available, there is ample space for all our players to participate in games. Some players, however, choose to spend these days working on individual fundamentals.

The results of this program can be measured by individual improvement as well as team success. We at Deer Park High School have found that this program allows each of our players to develop to the extent that he desires.

2

H. W. Thistlewaite

Head Basketball Coach
Princeton Junior High School
Youngstown, Ohio

BASIC CONDITIONING DRILLS

H. W. Thistlewaite has been coaching basketball at Princeton Junior High School since 1969. His overall record is 89 wins against 28 losses and includes three City Championships (1970-1971-1972) and one runner-up (1969).

All too often a basketball game is lost in the closing minutes because the team has become tired, the players' reflexes have slowed down and as a result their entire game pattern suffers.

Note: It has been my observation that some coaches do not spend enough time on conditioning and drills as the season progresses. They take conditioning into account in the beginning of the season but forget about its importance as the season wears on.

It's my belief that to have a successful team every year and thereby increase your chances for championships, you have to emphasize drill and conditioning throughout the season. This is not to say that you spend half your practice time on these aspects—but rather budget your time so there's room for them in your daily program.

191

Tip: I have my squad run wind sprints every other day to help build stamina. In addition, each member of the team jumps the bench while the rest of the team is warming up for the day's practice.

BENCH JUMPS

This drill must be performed daily to build the players' calves and thighs. In the early part of the season, I have the players do 20 jumps. We progress gradually, increasing by 10's until we are doing 50 a day. This drill not only builds the leg muscles but also contributes to the player's agility. The bench should be approximately 20 inches high and 14 inches wide.

Execution: The player jumps from one side to the other without stopping until he does the required amount. This simple drill will greatly increase the jumping ability of every player on the team.

REBOUNDING AND FOULING DRILL

Along with bench jumping I also have a rebounding drill that will put this jumping ability to practical use. We call this the rebounding and fouling drill. Its purpose is to teach the importance of board domination and concentration on making the shot when fouled, as well as going up with the shot after rebounding without dribbling. This will also create more three-point situations.

Execution: See Diagram 1 for drill setup. Team one will compete against team two, and the team that scores 12 points first wins. The losers must run ten laps and return for a rematch after the other teams have participated.

The rules are as follows:
1. No dribbling.
2. No passing.
3. Fouls allowed in moderation.

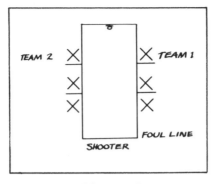

Diagram 1

4. No out-of-bounds.
5. Shoot until someone makes the shot.
6. Play resumes at the foul toss after the field goal has been attempted.

SHOOTING PRACTICE

Shooting requires practice just like any other phase of basketball. When players are shooting poorly there is a reason. By working with players individually you will be able to correct shooting errors.

Note: At the start of the season, my players practice shooting for a half hour of each practice session. During this time I take notes and later work with those who need correction.

Some of the common shooting errors are as follows:

1. Not looking at the basket when shooting under pressure.
2. Not looking the ball through the basket.
3. Holding the shooting arm too straight.
4. Shooting off balance—weight too far right or left; weight going away from the basket, resulting in loss of accuracy.
5. Not putting enough arch on shot.
6. Using too much of the palm instead of finger control.

● *Guards:* When working with the guards I try to emphasize these basic moves:

1. Shooting off a dribble.
2. Giving a good head fake and shooting.
3. Varying dribbling speed to set up a shot.
4. Working for high-percentage shots.

● *Forwards:* We stress shooting as well as rebounding ability for the forwards. By having a sound attack from your forwards and guards, you have a solid framework from which to work.

I teach the forwards several basic shooting situations and generally they can score by using one of these or a combination:

1. Head fake and shot.
2. No fake and shot.
3. Fake one way and shoot the other.
4. Hook shot—it's coming back into prominence.
5. Two quick fakes and a shot.
6. Drive and shoot.

Note: These situations are set up by using a one-on-one with a man playing a tough defense. Another good practice is to use two-on-two to create teamwork. I often work one-on-one with a player so I can show him what he is doing wrong and how he can correct it.

In these various ways, we build confidence in the player and thereby increase his efficiency. To get the better shot, the ball has to be gotten into good position either by a pass or by dribbling. In this instance, we will cover some dribbling drills.

DRIBBLING DRILLS

Here are two favorite dribbling drills that help our program:

● *Eyes off:* There are two ways to perform this drill. One way is by using blinders purchased from sporting goods stores, or by using shot glasses with the bottom halves of the

lenses painted black to limit vision. In this way, you see everything that goes on except the dribbling of the ball.

Note: Players on offense use these in a slowdown type of basketball play, with emphasis on dribbling ability.

• *Pivot dribble:* This is an excellent drill for improving a
player's dribbling ability. Set up two chairs as shown in Diagram 2, about eight feet from each other. The player dribbles from mid-court to the first chair. He pivots on his left
foot protecting the ball with his body and dribbles backward
to the next chair. When he reaches it, he pivots again on his
left foot, thereby putting him in forward motion toward the
basket for a layup.

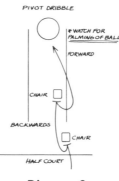

PIVOT DRIBBLE

WATCH FOR PALMING OF BALL

FORWARD

CHAIR

BACKWARDS

CHAIR

HALF COURT

Diagram 2

Note: The purpose of this drill is to teach dribbling control and enable the player to out-maneuver the defensive man. The coach must be able to demonstrate the correct pivots and to make certain the player is not palming as he makes his pivots.

CONCLUSION

When sound drills and good conditioning are built into
your program, you will find that your players will become
more aggressive and better able to compete throughout the
entire contest. Drilling and conditioning should go hand in
hand with a basic offense and defense.

3

Bill Hill

Head Basketball Coach
Clark Community College
Vancouver, Washington

COMBINING CONDITIONING AND SKILL DRILLS

Bill Hill coached high school basketball for the past fourteen years, compiling an overall record of 216 wins against 92 losses with five trips to the state tournament. The following article is based on his work at Battle Ground (Washington) High School. Bill Hill is now coaching at Clark Community College.

We attribute a good part of our basketball success at Battle Ground High School to the constant improvement of basic drills. All of the drills we use are keys to the winning tradition.

Note: In this article I'll concentrate on three drills which are favorites for various reasons.

The first is the Maze drill and it's my favorite. It combines basic skills and conditioning in balance so you don't waste time on conditioning alone. It is really a unique drill. When you try it, I know you will be a believer as I am.

The second is the 11-Man Continuity drill, and it is the players' favorite. It also combines conditioning and skills. With this drill, we emphasize one skill each evening—passing, aggression, outlet pass, blocking off the boards, etc.

Note: While this is a very standard drill, the key to making it good is the emphasis on one or two skills each night.

The third drill is the Attention drill and is liked by no one. But it serves the purpose of cleaning carbon from the soul and getting the players' attention so they can learn. And it will get their attention.

THE MAZE DRILL

This drill is set up as shown in Diagram 1.

1. Drill starts by sliding and pivoting from point A in square around the three-second area—then diagonally across the bottom diagonal. Pivot at each corner.
2. Sprint to the board and touch the bottom edge five times, or as high as you can jump.

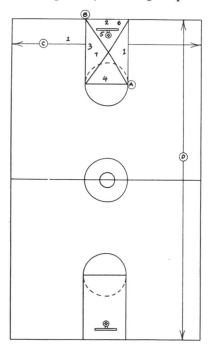

Diagram 1

3. Sprint to the nearest sideline and touch three and one-half widths of the floor.
4. Pick up ball waiting in the corner; dribble down and back the length of the floor. Time stops as you cross the end line.

Keys to the drill are these:

- Hit every corner with foot; add one second for every failure.
- Run two players at the same time from opposite ends.
- Use score clock and run down from one minute.
- Get squad involved and clock them. Our record is 41 seconds.
- You must execute the drill at full speed to get the value.

Purpose: The Maze drill provides sprinting, dribbling, pivoting, jumping, mental conditioning—and it promotes team pride.

ELEVEN-MAN CONTINUITY DRILL

The 11-man Continuity drill is set up as shown in Diagram 2. We come down 3-on-2:

1. Set triangle and move the ball—point stays at foul line.
2. One shot only.
3. All five players rebound.
4. Player getting the rebound hits nearest hook man, fills a lane with opposite hook man, and comes back the other way 3-on-2.
5. Players left behind fill spots and get ready.
6. Any number of players can be used by employing them at the hook positions.

Purpose: This drill is good for fast break fundamentals and conditioning. All the skills needed in game conditions are there. It's a matter of what skill you wish to emphasize that particular turnout. It is always the players' favorite drill.

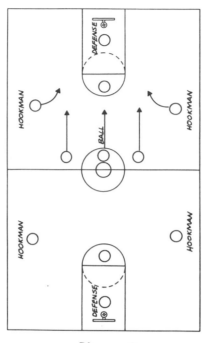

Diagram 2

ATTENTION DRILL

The Attention drill is set up as shown in Diagram 3.

1. The players face the coach and jump and reach as directed.

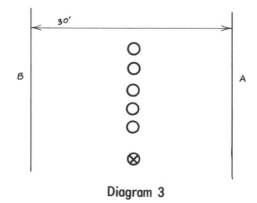

Diagram 3

2. On the whistle, they slide to lines A and B, touching them twice with one hand on the floor.
3. The player getting back to the middle first stands until the last player in the line has completed the drill, then he starts again.

Purpose: This is a good conditioning drill, both mentally and physically. Players seem to listen better after executing the drill.

4   Nick Creola

Head Basketball Coach
Jamestown Community College
Jamestown, New York

CONDITIONING: KEY TO MODERN BASKETBALL

As head basketball coach at Jamestown Community College, Nick Creola has a six-year record of 133 wins against 40 losses. He has been named Region III Coach-of-the-Year twice (1974-75; 1975-1976). Two of his teams (1973-74; 1974-1975) took National Scoring honors with 104 and 102 points respectively.

In the modern-day version of basketball with all the varieties of presses from the full-court press to the half-court press, it is imperative that a player be in the best possible condition before and during the season. Thus, the key to modern basketball is conditioning.

Note: At Jamestown Community College we are not blessed with height, so we depend on a strong weight program to aid our players.

CONDITIONING PROGRAM

In conditioning the basketball player, you should keep the following points in mind:

203

● Do not try to get the player in condition too quickly. It should be a gradual process, which is important to the player's health.

● Do not use running as a form of punishment. In this way, you discourage running rather than encouraging it.

● Do not cheat the player. Be fair and honest with him. It's more helpful to the boy and to you as his coach.

Note: Keeping these points in mind, we developed a conditioning program for our players to use before the season starts. Usually, we begin the program around the first week of September and finish it around the middle of October.

WEIGHT PROGRAM

Our weight program is run on a three-day basis with a day of rest in between each workout. In our program, we are primarily interested in building strength and endurance. We concentrate on both the legs and arms—for the reason that you need strength and endurance for both running and shooting.

Note: The following exercises are used and seem to meet the needs of our basketball players.

LEG SPLITS

● *Starting position:* Place the bar on the boy's shoulders. Use weights that are equal to one-third of his body weight.

● *Movement:* Do leg splits by putting one foot ahead of the other, then back. Continue this process until you have performed ten repetitions. In our program the players do three sets of ten repetitions, but on the last set they do as many as possible.

Note: This provides plenty of thrusting power, which is essential in basketball. The players continue this program for six weeks, adding five pounds for each preceding exercise period. One period consists of one day.

TOE RAISES

- *Starting position:* The player should stand with his feet shoulder-width apart, with the toes on a 2" by 4" board. The bar should be held behind the player's head and on his shoulder. Again, use one-third of his body weight.
- *Movement:* The player rises on his toes and returns to his heels. He should perform three sets of ten repetitions, again doing as many as possible on the last set. Add five pounds for each exercise period.

CURLS

- *Starting position:* Exercise from the standing position. Have the player hold the bar with his hands shoulder-width apart. Make sure his elbows are close to his body.
- *Movement:* Flex the arms and then extend the arms back into original position. Do three sets of ten repetitions, again doing as many as possible on the last set. Add five pounds to each exercise period.

TRICEP EXTENSION

- *Starting position:* The player should stand with the bar held behind his neck and his hands in a pronated position. The hands should be shoulder-width apart.
- *Movement:* Extend the arms above the head and then back into regular position. Start players off with twenty pounds of weight. Again, do three sets of ten repetitions, doing as many as possible on the last set. Add two pounds to each workout.

PUSH-UPS

- *Starting position:* Have player take push-up position on his finger tips.

● *Movement:* Have the player do as many push-ups as possible on his fingertips for twenty-five seconds. Rest one minute and continue this same process. On the last set, do as many fingertip push-ups as possible with no time limit. The push-ups are also done for three sets.

CONCLUSION

I have used this conditioning program for the past seven years in coaching both high school and junior college basketball players. The simplicity and time factor make this program worthwhile for all coaches. The players enjoy it and the results are worthwhile.

Dave Hadaway

Head Basketball Coach
John Adams High School
South Bend, Indiana

DRILLS TO CONDITION
THE INDIVIDUAL

Dave Hadaway's seven-year record as head basketball coach at John Adams High School is 129 wins against 40 losses, and includes five Northern Indiana Conference Championships; three South Bend City Championships; three sectional championships; one regional championship; one state tournament runner-up. Coach Hadaway has produced seven High School All-Americans in seven years.

It becomes more apparent each year that basketball games are won or lost on strength and quickness. Strength and quickness, although innate traits, can be improved with the use of proper drills and exercises aimed at long-range development.

Note: In Indiana, we are allowed to begin basketball practice on October 1 of each year. We play our first game around the end of November. This gives us seven to eight weeks of pre-season practice, in which to prepare our youngsters for perhaps the toughest schedule in the state.

We have used this pre-season period to great advantage

in not only increasing physical power and quickness, but also in setting a tempo for our season of discipline and dedication.

OUR PROGRAM

Our practices begin each day with a series of drills we have termed "The Ritual." We use the ritual when the team comes out on the floor at the beginning of practice. By so doing, we establish the tempo for that practice and because of freshness get more from the drills.

> Purpose: The purpose of the ritual is to improve and develop jumping ability, strength, agility, toughness, and overall physical condition. The drill creates a disciplined atmosphere of hard work and total commitment.

The ritual is divided into two segments—one part for the big men or "under the basket" people, and the other part for the outside men or wings and point men. The two groups run their specific drills separately but simultaneously.

The series of drills lasts less than ten minutes and is led by an assistant coach, using a whistle and stop watch. The individual starts the series on the whistle and goes until he hears it again. He then has fifteen seconds to prepare himself for the next segment.

> Note: We discontinue use of the ritual after the season begins on days before games. All players are encouraged to work at the ritual during the off-season, along with an intensive weight program.

THE RITUAL

This segment is for the "inside" players:
- *Rim touch* (30 times): The big men spread out at the various baskets and touch the highest part of the rim or board they can reach—30 times in a continuous motion. It is most important that they maintain balance and go straight up again as soon as they return to the floor.

• *Tipping* (30 times with each hand): The tipping drill is executed with the "under the basket" people tipping the ball against the board in a continuous motion. On the whistle they will tip 30 times with the left hand, stopping only when they have reached 30. They will then repeat the drill with the right hand.

> Note: It is important that the tip is executed with the fingertips, using a pushing motion toward the board and not a slap. Another important fundamental to stress is tipping the ball at the peak of the jump.

• *George Mikan drill* (2 minutes): This drill is very effective in developing hand-foot coordination in young players. The individual picks a spot on the board and lays the ball on that spot. He then catches the ball out of the net and executes the same maneuvers with the opposite hand. He performs these short hook-layup shots with no dribble.

> Tip: He always leaves the floor from the inside foot and steps into or toward the basket, keeping the ball above the shoulders throughout the drill.

• *Two-man continuous* (2 minutes): The purpose of the two-man continuous drill is to develop the ability to stay with the play until the ball is in the hole. The drill is also a great conditioner and instills toughness.

Two men stand a step out from the hole shoulder to shoulder facing the basket. The coach throws the ball up and they go until they hear the whistle. The only rule followed is no dribble. As soon as the ball is rebounded, a power move is executed back up to the hole. If the shot is made, the ball is taken out of the net and put up again; tipping is naturally encouraged before the catch.

> Note: Using the body for position is stressed along with the jab step and spinning to obtain rebounding position. Defensive blocking out, plus keeping the hands up on defense, are also demanded.

• *Bench jump* (2 minutes): This is a great drill to develop agility and jumping ability. An ordinary bench is used with the individual standing beside the bench with his side parallel to the bench. The player jumps back and forth across the bench until he hears the whistle, always keeping his side along the bench and not facing it.

> Tip: If benches are not available, one may purchase an elastic rope called a Chinese Jump Rope. It is much safer than a wooden bench and can be adjusted to various heights.

• *Dunking drill:* We also use a dunking drill for the players who are able to slam it through. We demand that they dunk ten times in a continuous motion, first with the left hand, then the right hand, and then with both hands. They are not allowed to stop until they execute the predetermined number.

> Note: It is a fine idea to call time out during a one-on-one drill or some other individual teaching situation and have the players execute this demanding drill. For the bigger boys, it's a fine way to get them to extend themselves and thus increase their jumping ability.

This second segment is for the "outside" players:

• *Jumping* (30 minutes): Because of a lack of baskets, we have our outside men jump and touch the highest part of the wall in a continuous motion. We stress the same fundamentals that we do with the big man jumping drill.

• *Skip passing drill* (30 times with each hand): Our guards pair off, face each other, and skip hook pass off the dribble thirty times with each hand. We stress skip passing with the ball coming up at a point just below the receiver's knees.

• *Inside-outside moves* (2 minutes): The outside men have their individual basketball; they dribble around the middle of the floor working at the inside look and going outside. They also work at the outside look, the cross dribble, and changing hands.

> Note: These are two very important moves, particularly in the open floor. We insist that all of our outside men perfect these two moves.

• *Dribbling* (2 minutes): All kinds of fancy dribbling are used. The outside men execute the change of pace and the stutter step. Two balls are also used—with one ball dribbled high and the other low.

• *Bench jump* (2 minutes): We also use the bench with the smaller players. In fact, all players on the squad, regardless of their physical development, can benefit from this drill which helps coordination.

BODY CONTROL DRILL

Balance and body control are certainly two of the most important and often overlooked skills for a young player to master. A vast number of errors and missed shots are caused at the high school level because of a lack of balance and sense of body control. A boy can't be a really good shooter without perfecting these skills.

We use a body control drill, five minutes per day, in the pre-season to help in this respect. All members of the squad line up along the sideline without a basketball, in what we term the "threat position"—that is, the feet are approximately shoulder-width apart with the back straight and the buttocks slightly above the knees.

The hands are carried at the throat or chest position as if the jump shot or a pass was to be executed. On command from the bench, they act out one of the following moves:

1. Jump shot.
2. Block a shot.
3. Tip.

They leave and return to the floor under control with the initial threat position maintained throughout the exercise. After we have executed the drill from a stationary position, we then act out the same three maneuvers from a running situation. We also use the command block, three shots, or take two jump shots with the idea of maintaining proper balance and body control throughout all movements.

Note: This simple drill instills the aspects of balance and body control. We believe in and constantly remind our players of the importance of body balance in all aspects of the game of basketball. Returning to this drill for a few short minutes throughout the season will continue to keep the importance of proper balance in the minds of young players.

EAGLE MAGIC DRILLS

Proper handling of the basketball is certainly one of the most important areas of development for any basketball player at any level. This past season, we averaged under ten errors per ball game throughout the nine-game state tournament, while scoring an average of 86 points per game during that period. In one ball game, we scored 90 points and had but 8 errors; in another game, we scored 87 points and had just 6 errors.

Note: This fine ball control can be directly related to the time we spent on a group of ball handling drills we have termed "Eagle Magic." The John Adams "Eagles" execute the nine ball handling drills, which make up the Eagle Magic, 15 to 20 minutes every day in pre-season practice. We also use the basketball handling drills 10 minutes per day on Mondays and Tuesdays after the season begins, and encourage our boys to spend some time on them daily during the off-season.

Each player has his own basketball for the drills. The drills are initiated with all players lining up along one sideline with their toes on the black line. The drills begin on command of a coach and continue for approximately one minute. We execute each of the drills twice.

The Eagle Magic drills accomplish three basic things —which are most important:

- They make a young player sensitive to the ball.
- They give him confidence.
- They create a disciplined yet enjoyable atmosphere in practice.

The ball handling drills are as follows:
- *Pincher:* Palm of hand faces player with ball resting on

the fingertips. The elbow is straight with arm up in front of face. Player squeezes ball up with fingertips in a continuous motion and changes hands every few seconds.

• *Drop and grab:* Begin with knees bent, back straight, and ball held directly in front of the body at knee level. Drill is started with ball brought in front of right leg and behind and dropped or bounced on the floor. The ball is then caught between the legs off the bounce and brought behind the left leg and in front and around right leg with same procedure continued.

• *Catcher:* Knees are bent straight back with ball held in front of the knees. Player flips the ball between legs and catches it by bringing hands to outside and in back of body. He then flips the ball in front and catches it.

Note: Drill continues in this manner in a motion as fast as the player can catch and flip.

• *Dribble around:* Player dribbles ball around each leg as fast as he can using short dribble. Do not allow the boys to look at the ball. Bend at knees with back held straight.

• *Shift and grab:* Player takes a stride stance, right foot ahead of left foot with ball held between legs. The right hand is on the outside of the leg and left hand is in between the legs. Player drops ball and shifts feet while catching ball before it hits the floor—by bringing left hand around the outside of his left leg and right hand between legs. He continues in this manner with shift and grab.

• *Around the world:* With the player's feet close together and body erect, the ball is circled as fast as possible up and down the length of the body from head to the ankles.

• *Bouncer:* Body is rigid with legs spread and ball held in front of the player. He bounces the ball between his legs and catches the ball in back by bringing hands around the outside of his body. He then bounces it from in back and catches it in front.

• *Inside-outside walk:* Ball is brought between legs and under right leg as the player walks or runs. It continues around the outside of the right leg and in between legs and around behind the left leg. When the group reaches the far sideline, they turn and come back. On the way back across, the ball is brought to the outside of the right leg and behind and in between legs and in front of the left leg and behind.

- *Two-man pass drill:* The entire squad sprints to endline where they execute the two-man pass drill the length of the floor. One ball is used for every two players. They use the defensive slide position in executing the drill while staying free-throw lane width apart. As soon as they hit the end line at the far end of the court, they drop the ball and sprint to sideline and come back in the "ape drill." On the ape drill, they slide backwards on angles; take three steps, hit the floor and change directions.

CONCLUSION

The drills discussed in this article are basic to our success at John Adams High School. We begin the various drills at the freshman level and continue them through the senior year. A greater amount of time is devoted to them in the freshman and sophomore years. Each individual is encouraged to continue the drills during the off-season.

All of the exercises can be executed by a youngster on his own without the guidance of a coach.

       Peter Mathiesen

Head Basketball Coach
California State University
Chico, California

CONDITIONING DRILLS FOR FUNDAMENTAL PLAY

Peter Mathiesen has been coaching high school and college basketball for the past fifteen years. His overall record is 247 wins against 176 losses, and includes two Far Western Conference Championships (1973-74; 1975-76). He was named Coach-of-the-Year in the Far Western Conference for the 1975-76 season.

Whether you're a high school coach with fifteen days of practice before the first game, or a college coach with fifty, you never seem to have enough time to prepare. With this in mind, we stress a few basic drills that if repeated almost daily will meet our offensive and defensive needs—yet allow us time to prepare for the press, the stall and various other things most teams have to face.

Note: The type and number of drills will be determined by the type of game you decide to play. We play a control game with continual pressure defense—thus we use drills that will help us in this respect.

● *Organized practice sessions:* We have a series of basic drills that we use almost every day. You may of course insert other drills, as we do once in a while, but we feel it's necessary to have a basic series that is timed and organized. Our organized practice sessions are no longer than one hour and forty-five minutes a day.

> Note: We begin each practice with fifteen minutes of circuit training which includes tipping, isometric work, dribbling, free throws, passing and jumping rope. We then go into our basic drills and conclude with team offense and defense as needed. We keep our gym open before and after practice for individual work.

DRILL PROGRAM

● *Footwork and stance drill:* We begin our drill program with a footwork and stance drill. This is the standard drill in which the coach directs the group to move left or right, up or back. We spend some time having the boys come to a quick stop and check their balance. As always, this serves as a conditioner, both mentally and physically.

● *Dribbling drill:* Our dribbling drill incorporates dribbling with our footwork and stance drill. We split the group into four sections (Diagram 1). The boy on defense puts his hands behind his back while the other boy dribbles the ball reversing direction as he goes from side to side within the contained area.

Going at half-speed, they switch positions at the end of the court and return to the starting position. After each boy goes through this, we have them use their hands, palms up, pointing the ball, going at full speed. Should the dribbler, who uses his free arm to protect the ball, beat the defensive man, he stops and allows him to catch up. They switch positions at the end of the court and return. Should the defensive man bat the ball away, he returns it to the offensive man and they continue.

> Note: As in all our drills, we stress pressure more than the interception or steal. We want to force the offensive man into a control error for two reasons—they lose possession, but more important, it creates mental uneasiness.

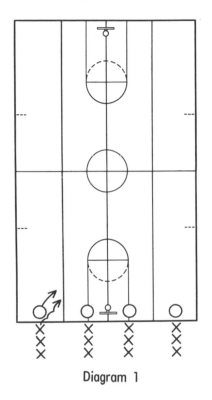

Diagram 1

● *One-on-one drill:* Diagram 2 illustrates our one-on-one drill. A boy will stay on defense until he steals the ball, gets the rebound, or causes a turnover. We stress rebounding position, defensive work and aggressiveness.

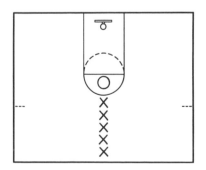

Diagram 2

Closeout drill: We then move into our one-on-one closeout drill (Diagram 3). A passes ball to B and sprints about halfway to ball, then assumes defensive stance and closes out on offensive man. Drill is not over until B scores or A obtains possession of the ball. When this happens they go to end of opposite lines.

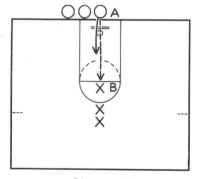

Diagram 3

● *Contesting the lead pass drill:* Diagram 4 illustrates our contesting the lead pass drill. Players rotate clockwise. A passes to B as C contests the pass. In the drill we have C put his baseline foot forward so he can split his vision and see both man and the ball. A cardinal rule is that if you lose either, make sure it is the ball and not the man.

B may use any moves to shake and release for the pass.

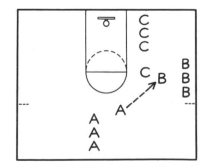

Diagram 4

We stop the drill as soon as B receives the ball or interception is made. On some days we continue the drill one-on-one after pass is received—for in all drills, we like to create a game-like situation.

- *Two-on-two drill:* We next go into the two-on-two drill (Diagram 5). Here we work on contesting the lead, pop switching, sliding and switching. We emphasize the pop switch, talking to teammates, aggressiveness—and keep this drill going until the offense scores or loses the ball. In all drills, we continue to work on rebounding and defensive footwork.

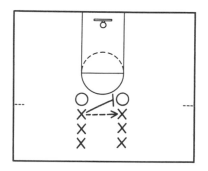

Diagram 5

- *Rebounding drill:* This drill (Diagram 6) stresses rebounding and helping out on defense. We go three-on-three

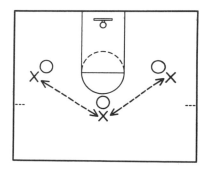

Diagram 6

utilizing those drills already described and have each boy call "shot" so his defensive partners can block out.

> Note: We will use this drill full court in order to go through all aspects of our game—including conditioning.

TEAM OFFENSE AND DEFENSE

From these drills we insert our offense and team defense. You may think we concentrate solely on defense—but in each of these drills we stress one-on-one moves, setting screens correctly and using them in the same manner, and offensive rebounding techniques. We feel that these basic drills complement our philosophy. They are basic basketball and we feel that this type of basic work wins games.

Our offense is built on the same fundamental philosophy. It's been our experience that a basic offense with proper execution of fundamentals will eventually lead to a high percentage shot. This also will allow you to control the tempo of the game—a very important ingredient in success.

> Variety of Offenses: We have used a variety of offenses over the past few years—and each has included give-and-go, screen and roll, and screen away techniques. Our out-of-bounds, jump ball and free-throw alignments have all been fundamental and successful. The out-of-bounds (Diagram 7) if executed properly is most successful—and it's easy to vary the direction of the cutters.

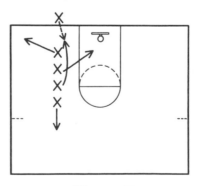

Diagram 7

In jump ball situations, there is always one open spot where you will have two men with no opponent between them. We work on tipping the ball here when we have the advantage—and when it is even or we are at a disadvantage, we go to the open spot of the opponent.

Our free-throw alignment (Diagram 8) is standard—for we are not concerned with a fast break off a missed shot; we want possession.

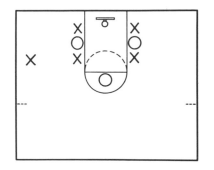

Diagram 8

Note: Team offense and team defense are widely discussed and always changing—but the fundamental aspects of the game stay pretty much standard. This is one of the main reasons for our philosophy.

7

Donald M. Jackson

Head Basketball Coach
Kalamazoo Central High School
Kalamazoo, Michigan

A PRE-SEASON CONDITIONING CIRCUIT

In nine seasons of Interscholastic coaching, Don Jackson has a winning percentage of 73.4%. In his first season at Msgr. John Hackett High School, he guided the Irish to the Class B State runner-up spot. In 1970 Coach Jackson moved to Kalamazoo Central High School where his squad reached the state finals. He has won two conference titles and several holiday tournament championships.

Most sports require the participants to attain a high degree of physical condition for maximum performance and efficiency. Coaches of endurance sports—basketball, soccer, wrestling, swimming, track— usually spend a great deal of practice time on conditioning activities. This is especially true prior to the competitive season.

Daily: Starting two or three weeks prior to actual practice, the prospective player in our basketball program should have a daily physical workout. This should be a lead-up activity with some basketball fundamentals and some activities that connote physical exercise. With this in mind, a circuit for basket-

ball was developed which is beneficial to prospective basketball players.

We have used a somewhat similar circuit in both the
pre-season football and baseball programs. On occasion a
varied circuit with intercom music has been used in small
physical education classes. In the past two seasons this type of
pre-season conditioning program, combined with an outside
running program in the fall, has helped our total operation
tremendously.

In implementing the circuit, during the first week of
conditioning all players are divided into groups of two and
are assigned to one of ten stations (fifteen stations can be
used if both varsity and junior varsity go through the circuit
at the same time). We allot two minutes to each station for
continuous activity; where it takes two players to accomplish
the activity, such as toe risers, each boy is active for one
minute.

Hustle: Movement in the circuit is in a clockwise manner, with
the coach's whistle directing change from station to station.
We stress hustle throughout the circuit and allow no time for
rest periods until the entire circuit has been completed. When
two or three weeks of circuit training are finished, opening
day of actual practice will find each player physically and
mentally ready to play basketball.

Diagram 1 illustrates the circuit with suggested activities, as follows:

1. *Jumping jacks or side-straddle hop.* Two traditional exercises.
2. *Push-ups, fingertip variety.* Develops fingers for
   shooting and ball-handling.
3. *Rope jumping, continuous.* Develops muscle group in
   legs.
4. *Toe risers, three-quarter squat with partner on back.*
   Develops muscles in legs.
5. *Running lane: forward sprints alternating with backward run.* Stops and starts also recommended.

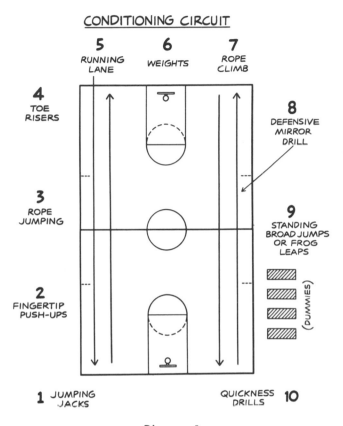

CONDITIONING CIRCUIT

Diagram 1

6. *Weights: two sets of wrist weights.* Each man rolls a weight up and down a cord attached to a 1½-foot length of broomstick. Player holds the weight away from him, wrist-rolls the weight up, then unwinds. An excellent wrist and forearm developer.

7. *Rope climb.* Another exercise or drill may be substituted but the rope climb is good for wrist and forearm development.

8. *Defensive mirror drill: one-on-one without the ball.* Work length of court in narrow lane: strive for containment, direction change. Ball added after first week.

9. *Standing broad jump or leap frogs.* Done over a series of football dummies.

10. *Quickness drills, for feet, hands, mind.* Use quarter turns, right and left slides, right and left oblique angle slides, forward and retreating slides, hands and arms up and down, various exercises.

Flexibility: This circuit can be very flexible. Other exercises and activities that we have used include: free throws (one man shoots, other retrieves), sit-ups, standing long jumps, continuous rim tips, continuous layups on spot under basket, weight lift curls, and dribble weave (around and between pylons).

8

Anthony Zanin

Head Basketball Coach
Haverford College
Haverford, Pennsylvania

PRE-SEASON TRAINING IDEAS FOR THE SMALL SCHOOL

Before taking over the head coaching spot at Haverford College, Tony Zanin coached at Ridgefield Memorial High School in New Jersey for four years, the "small school" described in the following article. During that time his teams posted a 61-18 mark and won two North Jersey Conference co-championships and placed second the other two years. In all four seasons his squads made the state tournament.

Coaching at a small school for the past four years, I have found myself lacking not only a big man, but overall team height. Because of this lack of height we have depended a great deal on team quickness, excellent jumping ability, aggressiveness and excellent conditioning.

We have dedicated most of our pre-season practices toward developing the above abilities. A great deal of our quickness and jumping skill has come from the use of agility drills and the Exer-geni. Our aggressiveness has come from the attitude of the players toward the game and from a number of contact drills used in practices.

PRE-SEASON

During the first two weeks of our pre-season drills, practice sessions have been divided into four sections:

• *First:* Players report onto the floor for a prescribed shooting drill which covers the types of shots that they will be taking during a game. During these shooting drills they also do their individual work on the Exer-geni. Three different drills are used on the Exer-geni to develop certain abilities. To develop the muscles of the legs, used for jumping, we use bicycle and scissor exercises (Diagram 1). Then two players at a time use the long line harness on the Exer-geni, doing three repetitions of ten seconds each; this helps build up leg endurance.

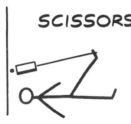

Diagram 1

At another section of the floor we have a second long line harness Exer-geni hooked up to the flying rings and raised to about eleven feet. At the end of the harness is a basketball tied in a net. We have a manager regulate the pressure by holding the free end of the harness. The basketball is raised to an appropriate height for each player— usually from 9' 6" on up. The player takes one step, jumps and grabs the ball with both hands and pulls it down. He repeats this about ten times; this helps get the player used to pulling down a rebound against pressure.

AGILITY DRILLS

● *Second:* The court is divided into ten areas with each area serving as an agility drill station:

1. Jumping rope.
2. Jumping and tapping ball against wall with right hand.
3. Jumping and tapping ball against wall with left hand.
4. Moving ball in and out of legs in figure-eight fashion.
5. Tire drill—two tires, one placed on top of the other. Player jumps with alternate foot touching each time (Diagram 2).

TIRE DRILL

Diagram 2

6. Tire drill—two tires alongside each other. Player jumps from one tire to the other with both feet touching down within tire.
7. Moving ball from hand to hand behind back.
8. Ball drill—player stands with back to manager, who yells "Ball!" and throws ball at turning player, who must catch it.
9. Rope drill—a piece of rope tied about two feet above the floor. Player jumps over rope sideways, touches ground and jumps back.
10. Line drill—player straddles mid-court line, jumps up, turns around and and lands facing in opposite direction.

For agility drills each player occupies a station; at a given signal they begin their drills, doing each drill for 30 seconds. These drills are done with constant touch-and-go movement at top speed for the full time. Players rotate from drill to drill until they cover all ten drills. Not only do the drills develop agility but they are also a tremendous conditioner.

RUNNING SKILLS

● *Third:* A number of running drills improve conditioning and also develop specific offensive and defensive skills. We start off with two defensive drills:

1. Slide-step around court. The players assume a low defensive stance with hands spread wide. They take long slide steps sideways, moving around the outer edge of the court, first to their right and then their left.
2. Container drill. Player assumes low defensive position while offensive player dribbles ball at him. Defensive player retreats, using back-step with a wide foot base and always having one foot in front of the other, never letting feet get caught up. Drill is done up and down the court with players rotating at each end.

Offensive running drills:

1. Dribble relays. Player dribbles ball down court with right hand and back with left hand.
2. Two-man passing relays. Ball is passed back and forth between two players going down the floor and back.
3. Figure-eight relay.
4. One-man fast-break drill. Manager stands on foul line and rolls ball toward opposite basket. Player must run after ball, pick it up and lay it into the basket.

It should be noted that all of the above drills are to be done at top speed.

TEAM DRILLS

● *Fourth:* A number of team drills utilize both offensive and defensive abilities, which are extremely helpful in our man-for-man defense and our offense against a man defense.

1. Block-out drill. Ball is placed on the floor, three defensive men triangle it and three offensive men stand behind them. At the whistle the defense tries to block out while the offense goes for the ball.

2. Scramble drill. We firmly believe that every loose ball should be ours so we work at getting it. Two lines are formed on either side of a manager, who rolls ball out while one player from each line goes after the ball, trying to retrieve it before the other player.

3. One-on-one full court. The offensive player tries to beat the defensive man going toward the opposite basket. The defender scrambles to get in front of the offensive man and constantly forces him back toward the other side of the floor.

4. Two-on-two full court. The offense works on give-and-go options and setting good offensive screens. The defense works on switching, forcing men to go behind—and then dropping back into the middle.

5. Three-on-three full court. Same principles as in the two-on-two drill.

6. Three-on-two full court. Offense works on controlled fast break while defense works on getting back in tandem defense to stop break or slow it down.

Practice sessions are divided into the above four parts for the first two weeks of practice; after that, we keep using the Exer-geni and agility drills but drop the other drills in favor of the more advanced materials we use during the season. We stop using the Exer-geni and agility drills once the season begins.

SOME QUESTIONS

● *Why are all of the drills done at top speed?* We believe that basketball is a game of pressure, and the team which reacts best to the pressure on both defense and offense will win its share of games regardless of the amount of talent they have.

● *Do we have time to work on all of these things during a single practice session?* Yes. You may spend as much or as little time on each drill as you like. A breakdown of our 2½-hour practice: Part 1, 30 minutes; Part 2, 25 minutes; Part 3, 35 minutes; Part 4, 60 minutes.

● *Do you continue these drills once the season starts?* There are various feelings on this but we don't continue them. We have found that through high-speed practices and games we maintain the qualities we've gained in our pre-season practices.

All of the drills not only are conditioners, but also develop specific skills in each player; these skills help a team execute properly during a game. A team that is small cannot afford mistakes during a game; that is why we work so hard on offensive and defensive execution and on being in better physical condition than our opponents. The proof was the consistency with which we outscored our opposition during the second half of our games; we attribute this imbalance to our excellent conditioning, enabling us to exert constant pressure on the opposition throughout the entire game. The major part of this conditioning came in our pre-season work.

Head Basketball Coach
Northeast Louisiana University
Monroe, Louisiana

PRE-SEASON AND EARLY-SEASON BASKETBALL PREPARATION

Lenny Fant, Northeast Louisiana University's head coach since 1957, is one of college basketball's leading winners with 330 victories for twenty-three seasons at Louisiana College, East Texas Baptist and NLU. He has a string of fifteen consecutive winning seasons at Northeast. His overall college record is 330-233 and his nineteen-year mark at NLU is 268-196.

Our pre-season and early-season drills are designed to build the stamina, muscular control, and agility that will be needed during the regular season. At Northeast Louisiana State College we have developed several excellent drills that will help players prepare for the basketball season.

PRE-SEASON CONDITIONING

Two weeks prior to the opening of fall workouts, which begin on October 15th, we get our squad on the track, dividing them into three groups.

1. The tall group: 6'5" and up.

2. The middle group: 6'3" to 6'5".
3. The short group: under 6'3".

There are usually about eight kids in each group. They will start running on the back-side of the 440-yard track and run ten 220's a day. They run in their groups, and we have a recorder to record each time that is run. They will then walk the remainder of the track, 220 yards, and be ready to run again.

> Note: We average each day's ten runs individually, and then we average the group. Each group is competing against the other group. Our goal is to average 29 seconds for the short group, 30 seconds for the middle group, and 31 seconds for the tall group. We find that it gets competitive, group against group, and after the first three days they really put out. We have a two-mile relay (with baton) on the tenth day. Each boy will run a 440 and compete with his group.

Because of these pre-season drills, when we hit the floor for our first day's early-season workout, we have no trouble with conditioning. Each boy can go full speed, having had good leg and wind conditioning.

EARLY SEASON

When we get into the gym on October 15th, we start each day's work with seven minutes of exercise. Most of the exercises we do are for the legs. All of them are done on the four-count. They are done quickly, going from one right into the next.

● *Exercises:* Exercises are done in the order indicated below.

Side-straddle hops	Half knee-bends
Touch toes	Leg lifts (from back position)
Body bends	Push-ups
Jump arounds	Come up running in place

We do this only the first two weeks.

Note: These exercises are done with one of the older boys leading. Everyone else lines up abreast in four lines.

• *Ropes:* We go from the exercises into four minutes of rope jumping, the last minute at full speed. The boys become very good at the ropes and get to the point where they can cross their hands, jump once and let the rope go under twice, jump backwards, and really make the rope hum with their jumping speed. This is one of the best agility drills that we know.

We stay with the ropes well into the season. Sometimes, for a change of pace, we substitute shadow boxing for rope jumping. The ropes are very good for hands-feet coordination and conditioning.

• *Piggyback:* Some 15 years ago, we adapted the late Buckey O'Connor's weight overload theory on building legs to our basketball program. After trying three sets of weights with different poundages for different size boys, we found that this was too time-consuming. We then decided to pair the boys off into groups of two and let each boy carry the other on his lower back, the full length of the floor and back.

We have the boy who is carrying try to walk in a ⅛ to ¼ knee bend and get on his toes as much as possible. We can do this drill in a very short time because everyone is drilling together.

• *Bench jumps:* We have several 14- or 15-inch benches in our gym. Starting the first day, we jump these benches everyday. We can jump three people to the bench and have everyone jumping at the same time.

We start off the drill the first day with everyone jumping 25 times, the next day we will jump 28 times, the next day 31, and so forth, until we reach 50 jumps. We will hold at 50 repetitions for the balance of the year.

Note: We try to do these without a pause or a miss. This means we have to land with balance and jump high enough to clear the bench on each jump.

• *Jumping meter:* In 1955, when I was coaching at East Texas Baptist College, we realized a great need for a measur-

ing device that could measure the vertical jumps of our basketball players. We needed something that would measure
each jump and also permit the boys to jump quickly, so that it
could be worked into each day's practice period.

The device we invented was the jumping meter (Diagram 1). It consisted of 12 one-inch square pegs, which were
from 4 to 16 inches long. Each one was one inch longer than
the one after it. A one-inch space was also allowed between
each peg, making them one inch apart, too.

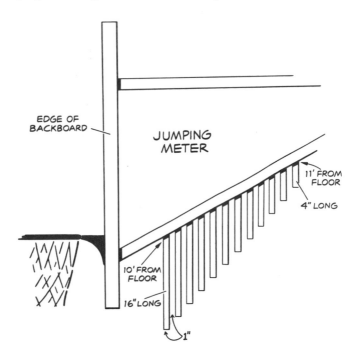

EDGE OF
BACKBOARD

JUMPING
METER

11' FROM
FLOOR

4" LONG

10' FROM
FLOOR

16" LONG

1"

Diagram 1

The longest peg was placed 10 feet from the floor, the
second peg was 10 feet 1 inch from the floor, the third peg
was 10 feet 2 inches, and so on to the shortest peg, which was
11 feet from the floor.

The original meter, which was placed on the side backboard support that comes down at an angle, was made of

wooden pegs. But, we found that these wooden pegs broke, over a period of years, due to the force of the slap or touch.

When our first meter broke, we replaced the broken pegs with heavy rubber truck tubing. This tubing is much more durable than wood, and it can be cut to the same dimensions as the wooden pegs. We fastened these tubes to our original structure, and we are using it still.

- *Peg jumps:* At first we did not let the players run and jump at the meter, but allowed them one step, simulating rebound situations. We found that they could jump a little higher if they got a running jump. They were still developing the same muscles and jumping ability; so, since the success of this drill depends on each boy putting the maximum effort into each jump every day, we let them take a running jump.

Each boy would jump a peg higher than he had already hit. If he did not hit the one he jumped at, he could still hit a lower one on each jump because the pegs are only one inch apart.

Note: We line our kids up and each one jumps three times. This gives us enough time to allow the entire squad to jump three times in about three minutes.

We don't know how high each one can jump, but they know. When one of them goes up a notch, everyone knows by that person's actions. The least improvement that we have had in a career totaled four inches, and the most totaled 11.

We are not certain what contributes most to the improvement of jumping ability, but we have tried to install all the known methods in our early practices.

WORTHWHILE EXERCISES

After 16 years, we find these four exercises have been well worth the time spent on them during practice:

- *Ropes:* For teaching coordination and building endurance.
- *Piggyback:* To develop the legs.
- *Bench jumps:* To teach repetition and develop balance.

- *Peg jumps:* To spark maximum effort and instill incentive.

We have had 5'9" and 5'6" boys who could dunk the ball. The 5'9" boy was the one who improved 11 inches.

After the first week or two, the boys' jumping height will go down; then it gradually goes up again. After a couple of days off, they can jump higher. You will see a great deal of improvement in the second year.

Note: We go right out of the three jumps into our first fundamental drill.

Former Head Basketball Coach
Barnwell High School
Barnwell, South Carolina

AN OFF-SEASON WORKOUT PROGRAM

As the former head basketball coach at Barnwell High School, Bob Whitehead compiled an overall record of 121 wins against 79 losses. He coached the South squad in the annual North-South All-Star Game (1975) and was a member of the Board of Directors of the South Carolina Basketball Coaches Association. Bob Whitehead retired from coaching in 1975.

We believe that one of the most important phases of a high school basketball player's career is the off-season workout program. During the regular season most of our work deals with preparation for our opponents with very little time available for individual work on fundamentals. Because of the time element, we tend to stress team workouts and neglect to allow time for important individual fundamentals. Because of these factors, we feel that a good off-season program that emphasizes individual fundamentals is a must for having a successful season, year after year.

STATION WORK

Our solution, after trying various methods, is station work. While writing this article, I realize that this method is not new, and I take no credit for the development and discovery of such. I do heartily recommend it as an excellent way to make off-season practice more interesting and enjoyable.

Our stations are designed to cover the basic fundamentals of basketball while keeping the interest as high as possible during the off-season when there is no immediate goal in sight. By setting up various stations and putting each player through them, we are touching on all of the basic fundamentals that we may have neglected during the season. We have found that our players remain very much interested during the off-season because each station offers a different challenge and is not long and drawn out. He doesn't have to wait for 10 or 15 players to go through the drill before he can go to something else. By repeating these stations at least three days a week, the players soon become adept at them.

EIGHT STATIONS

We divide the gym into eight stations, and put no more than four to a group at each station. You can keep 32 players active. Upon completion of a ten-minute workout, players rotate in a clockwise manner to the next station.

Note: We require our players to hustle to each station during the rotation.

After an hour and twenty minutes, each player has covered all of the basic fundamentals of basketball.

The coach moves throughout the stations. He signals, usually by blowing his whistle, the changing of stations after each time lapse.

Upon completion of station work, the players are allowed to choose teams and scrimmage free-lance to put what they have learned into game-type situations. The scrimmage lasts approximately 30 minutes. The workout is ended with a short period on the weights, stressing legs, shoulders, hands, and wrists.

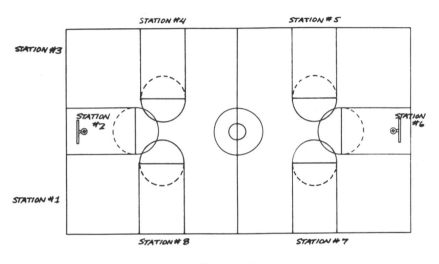

Diagram 1

EXPLANATION OF STATIONS

An explanation and a diagram (Diagram 1) of the stations follow.

Station #1:   Ropes
　　　　　　　a. forward and backward spot-jumping (keeping arms close to the body and using wrists)
　　　　　　　b. crossover
　　　　　　　c. box
　　　　　　　d. run while jumping

Station #2:   Tipping
　　　　　　　a. right-hand and left-hand tips off board
　　　　　　　b. two-hand tip off board
　　　　　　　c. work in pairs and tip ball across board and then in

Station #3:   Rebounding
                  a. Using McCall Rebounder or similar device, pull down 10 rebounds, increasing height each time
                  b. 25 pull-throughs (using both hands, pull ball through arm 25 consecutive times)

Station #4:   Take the charge
                  a. working one-on-one, each player must learn to let the offensive player charge into him. We teach players how to break fall, etc.

Station #5:   Dribbling (using blinders)
                  a. right-handed and left-handed dribbling
                  b. crossover
                  c. hesitation dribble
                  d. behind-back dribble
                  e. speed dribble

Station #6:   Shooting
                  a. Each player works on jump shot, hook, layup, set shot from respective positions in our offense

Station #7:   Passing
                  a. Working in pairs, players make every imaginable pass repetitiously.

Station #8:   Free-throw shooting
                  a. Each player shoots two free throws at a time and rotates. He must step from line between shots to get game setting.

11

Oscar Catlin

Physical Education Instructor
Lawson State Community College
Birmingham, Alabama

A SUMMER TRAINING PROGRAM

Oscar Catlin coached high school and college basketball for many years. His last assignment was head coach at Tuskegee (Alabama) Institute where his 1972 squad posted a 22-6 mark and captured the SIAC conference championship, which earned him the conference Coach-of-the-Year award. His overall coaching record (high school and college) is a most impressive 183-53. At present, he is a physical education instructor at Lawson State Community College.

The following is a summer training program that has proven successful for our basketball needs. The program is repeated in a faster pace come September when we add agility and quickness drills.

WEIGHTS

Work with weights two or three times per week.
• Warm-up before beginning.
• Repetitions 7 to 10 each set. Increase weights with each lift repetition. Lighter weight with 7 repetitions and heavier with 5.

● Work on the following: half squat; toe raises; hamstring exercise; biceps curl; military press; regular rowing; upright rowing adduction; abduction; circumduction; elevation; reverse curl; toe raise on 2″ × 4″; wrist curl.

RUNNING

Perform regular over-distance running (hill and road running) and cross-country running.

● *Monday:*
   A.M.—3 to 6 miles over-distance.
   P.M.—2 to 4 miles over-distance; speed-60's (15 to 20) at ½ and ¾ speed, with 30-yard jog intervals.
● *Tuesday:*
   A.M.—3 to 6 miles over-distance.
   P.M.—Repetitions (for staying power) 220's (8 to 10) at 25 seconds each, with 50-second intervals.
● *Wednesday:*
   A.M.—3 to 6 miles over-distance.
   P.M.—8 to 10 miles light over-distance.
● *Thursday:*
   A.M.—3 to 6 miles over-distance.
   P.M.—Repetition running (for staying power) 440's (5 to 10) at 55 to 57 seconds each, with 3- to 5-minute intervals, or 330's (5 to 10) at 34 to 36 seconds each, with 3-minute intervals.
● *Friday:*
   A.M.—3 to 6 miles over-distance.
   P.M.—3 to 4 miles light over-distance; light speed 2 to 3 sets of 60's (1 over 1), that is, no intervals, at ¾ speed.
● *Saturday:*
   A.M.—6 to 8 miles over-distance.
   P.M.—Rest.

SHOOTING BASKETBALL

Shoot for one hour a day with no competition. Practice the following: free throws; layups; floor shots; jump shots.

Note: Is there a secret to good shooting? It is countless hours of practice and more prcatice. Each man on the squad must be a shooter.

Here are some shooting hints to remember:

1. Always practice shots that will be taken in the game. It is foolish for the big center to spend time shooting from the guard position when he will never attempt these shots in the game.
2. Don't "force" the shot.
3. Learn to relax when shooting.
4. Never attempt "wild" or "crazy" shots.
5. Always follow-through
6. Don't shoot when a teammate is in better position.

Note: Shooting takes practice. You must be able to shoot the perfect shot and know where you shoot best from. See Diagram 1 for "area of practice."

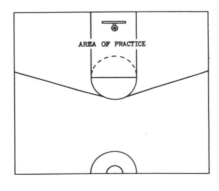

AREA OF PRACTICE

Diagram 1

12

Woody Williams

Director of Intramurals
Lebanon City Schools
Lebanon, Ohio

BASKETBALL DRILLS: CONDITIONERS FOR THE GAME

Woody Williams started coaching high school basketball in 1966 at Lucille Berry (Lebanon, Ohio) Junior High School. He then moved to Adena (Frankfort, Ohio) High School. His overall record is 49-29 and includes a conference title and a Coach-of-the-Year award. He is presently Director of Intramurals for the Lebanon City Schools.

The use of drills in basketball is an essential and integral part of one's success or failure in coaching the game. The philosophy of coaches as to what should be attained from a drill will vary with each individual coach and each individual drill.

Note: My thinking on the subject is very basic. You must use only the drills that will benefit your style of play and each drill should be spelled out to your team in such a way that they understand what you are trying to accomplish.

I have found in coaching at all levels that the players are

too willing to accept drills only as something that they have to do as a part of basketball—rather than realizing the benefits they can reap from understanding the elements within the drill that can bring them success.

DRILL PHILOSOPHY

Well-executed drills may not always bring success, but the percentage for accomplishment is going to be greater for those who work the hardest toward perfection. With this theory in mind, I try to establish the drills that will fit the type of players and the style of play that I will be teaching. In teaching the drill, I will point out the importance of each maneuver that the player will make in his execution of the drill.

> Note: All drills should be run with a great deal of spirit and at full speed. If a boy is allowed to loaf on a drill, how can he be expected to react in a game situation? I'm a great believer in the old adage, "You play the way you practice."

You, as the coach, must show spirit and enthusiasm as well as the players. If you are not enthused with your drills, it's pretty difficult to get your players in the proper frame of mind. One instrument I found to be a great help in keeping the spirits high during drills was to integrate music into my practice time, especially during drills. We also use music while free shooting and during free-throw work. We might even turn up the volume a little during the foul shooting so as to add a little distraction to the workout.

In running a drill, time is an important commodity. You should never run a drill for a long period of time. You will find that running several drills over a period of time will prove to be a better and more valuable teaching method than running one or two drills for a long period of time.

> Note: However, you must avoid running a number of vigorous drills back to back. Trying to get perfection out of extremely tired individuals can be detrimental to good teaching.

Drills must be planned in a desirable sequence. Follow vigorous drills with shooting drills, either field goal or free throw. We shoot at least 100 free throws each night and most are shot at periods following vigorous drills.

DRILL PROGRAM

I feel that through spirited, well-planned and well-executed drills a coach can develop a fundamentally sound ball club. You must keep in mind that the fundamentals must be taught constantly and taught well. This can be done through drills that are well executed.

Here are some drills that I have used during my coaching which have been very instrumental in what success my teams have enjoyed. They cover many phases of offensive and defensive basketball, and teach many of the techniques so important to the game.

• *Scramble drill* (Diagram 1): To start we divide our team into four equal groups and place them at the four corners of the gym floor as shown. We will letter the corners— A, B, C and D. We place one man from each line just outside the foul circle at the foul line extended.

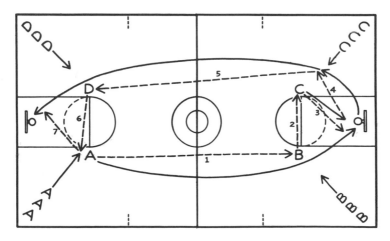

Diagram 1

The scramble starts with player A taking the ball and throwing a right-hand baseball pass down floor to player B and following his pass. Player B pivots and tosses player C a chest pass across the foul circle. With proper timing, C will feed player A a bounce pass as he cuts off player B at top speed for the layup.

Player C will rebound and fire player A an outlet pass as he continues on toward the end from which he originally started. After A has taken the pass he must pass to player D. Player D shovels a pass to a player who has taken A's starting position. The new player A gives the running A a bounce pass for the layup.

> Note: All players involved in the round just completed rotate clockwise. When we switch the drill and run it to the left, all passes and shots are made with the left hand and the rotation is counter-clockwise. We also run this drill with two basketballs. The timing must be precise and the players must move at top speed. It can also be run as a passing drill only; no dribbles are allowed and no shots are taken. We also throw a weighted ball in this passing drill from time to time.

• *Points to emphasize:* Timing and proper passing techniques are points to emphasize in this drill. A player must make the layup at both ends or he will run the drill again. Also, we make sure that the post players do not stand in the foul lane when waiting for the ball. They must stay outside the lane to avoid the three-second violation. Don't allow them to linger there in practice because they can't do it in a game.

• *Three-on-two, two-on-one drill* (Diagram 2): This drill is run full-court from three lanes we call A, B and C at one end of the court. At the other end of the court we have a two-man tandem defense that we call D1 and D2. Thus, we are set for the three-on-two attack.

Player B will start the play by making an outlet pass to either player A or player C with whom player B will change positions. This change is made as it is in a fast-break situation where there is the outlet pass then a filling of the three breaking lanes. The wing men must stay on the break.

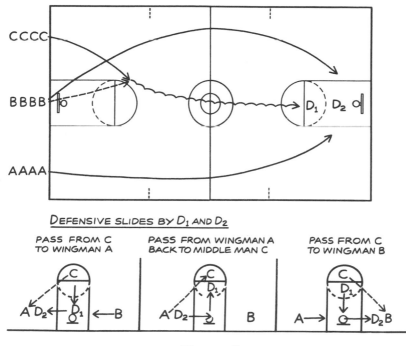

Diagram 2

We now have the three-on-two situation. As we attack the tandem defense, the middle man is not allowed to venture beyond the foul line unless he can drive all the way for the layup. The reason for his stopping at the line is to avoid cluttering the foul lane and thus allowing the tandem to defense all three offensive men more readily.

The tandem defense will stay in a straight line in the lane with D2 behind D1. The straight-line pattern will break when the middle man passes off to a wing man. When this happens, D2 will slide to the side to which the ball goes. D1 will slide straight back and fill the spot which D2 has vacated. The defensive area coverage will stay constant for these two men. D1 slides up and down the key area. D2 covers the baseline area from corner to corner.

• *Points to emphasize:* The points we emphasize on the three-on-two portion of this drill are these. Offensively, we want the three players to keep spread so as to present tough coverage for the tandem. We want the ball to be moved very quickly and the first good percentage shot to be taken. As for the defensive tandem, we want them to play the defense aggressively and force the offense to take the longest shot they can be forced to take. The tandem pair must do their defensive sliding quickly and correctly to avoid the layup.

The *change-over* from the three-on-two aspect to the two-on-one is done as follows: When a basket is scored by A, B or C or when D1 or D2 gets the ball through a rebound or steal, the pair who were the tandem become the two offensive men going toward the other goal. The player who comes down the floor from line C automatically becomes the single defensive man going back as a challenge for the pair coming down. Players A and B remain as the new tandem.

D1 and D2, now the offense, must stay wide so that player C is unable to cover both of them easily. Player C must not over-commit himself to either man. He must try to stop the ball but he must also avoid letting the second man get loose under the basket for a layup. The defense man must try to force the longest shot possible as the tandem defense did.

• *Bull-in-the-ring drill* (Diagram 3): For this drill we divide the squad into two circles consisting of six players for a twelve-man squad. A man is taken from the circle to become a defensive man within the circle. The defensive man chases the ball as the players around the perimeter pass it around. The ball may not be passed to a player on the immediate right or left of the passer. The ball also may not be passed over the head of the defender.

Note: When the defender forces a bad pass or touches a passed ball or has the ball thrown over his head, he is replaced by the player who threw the ball. This drill proves to be a good conditioner as well as a good teaching aid for pressure defense.

• *Points to emphasize:* We emphasize quick, sharp passes

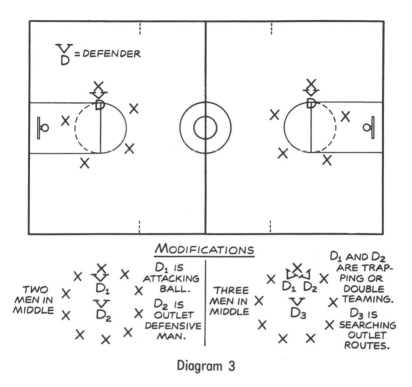

Diagram 3

by the perimeter players as well as quickness and good defensive techniques by the "bull in the ring." After a while we put both groups together to form one large circle and we put two defenders in the ring. Here we emphasize that one player aggressively attack the ball while the other tries to cut off possible passing outlets.

> Note: When the position of the ball changes, so do the assignments of the defensive men. You must emphasize that the man watching for the outlet pass not loaf while the attacking defender is working hard to force the bad pass.

We also put three men in the ring. When we do this we form a double-team with the two men near the ball while again the third man tries to sense the outlet passing lane. When the double-team is formed we emphasize the points of a profitable double team: attack the man with the ball; never reach or grab for the ball; let him make the mistake of either making a bad pass or holding the ball for the five-second count.

CONCLUSION

Drills are an important part of your team's success or failure. However, the success or failure aspects will come from the quality of your material and how well or how poorly the drills have been taught and received by your players.

Your players should never take a drill and its results for granted. Let them know what is expected from the drill and impress upon them the importance of the old adage, "You play the way you practice."